EXETER
A Roman Legionary Fortress and *Civitas* Capital

ARCHAEOPRESS ROMAN SITES

EXETER

A ROMAN LEGIONARY FORTRESS AND *CIVITAS* CAPITAL

JOHN PAMMENT SALVATORE

ARCHAEOPRESS ARCHAEOLOGY

ARCHAEOPRESS PUBLISHING LTD
Summertown Pavilion
18-24 Middle Way
Summertown
Oxford OX2 7LG
www.archaeopress.com

ISBN 978-1-80327-628-1
ISBN 978-1-80327-629-8 (e-Pdf)

Front cover by Archaeopress. Thanks to Wim Scherpenzeel (legionary of *Legio Secunda Augusta,* Nederland); Hans Splinter (photographer), and the estate of the late Peter Connolly (© akg-images/Peter Connolly).

This book is available direct from Archaeopress or from our website
www.archaeopress.com

For †Christopher (Chris) Henderson
and †Paul T. Bidwell

both formerly of Exeter Museums Archaeological Field Unit
without whom this book could never have been written

Videas bonas aves

Contents

List of Figures

Author's Note

In the Autumn of 2022, a chance conversation with Roger White, senior lecturer in archaeology at the University of Birmingham, was followed by discussions with David Breeze at the Roman Limes (Frontiers) Congress in Nijmegen Holland. I was subsequently offered the chance to write this book on Roman Exeter for the Archaeopress Roman sites series. Given my 50-year association with the archaeology of Roman Exeter I had no hesitation in accepting and am most grateful for the opportunity.

I arrived in Exeter from London in 1972, intending only a short stay whilst awaiting my first archaeological 'digging' post, a summer season at Dewlish Roman villa in the neighbouring county of Dorset. However, quite unexpectedly there arose the prospect of joining excavations in the city centre being carried out by the Exeter Museums Archaeological Field Unit. Initially signing up for six weeks, this fortuitous decision proved to be life-changing as I was very rapidly and expertly tutored in the techniques of urban multi-period open-area excavation by the late Christopher 'Chris' Henderson. I went on to stay in Exeter for 10 years beyond those first six weeks, during which I participated in numerous archaeological investigations within the city, many of which have provided the foundations for this book.

The arrival of qualified archaeologists at Exeter in the 1970s saw the development of innovative archaeological techniques which paved the way for a major breakthrough in the understanding of the origins of the city as a Roman military foundation. This book illustrates how the remarkable archaeological exposures from those early years of intense investigation built up a picture of the evolution of Roman Exeter, which was hitherto completely hidden from view. The archaeological work of the last decades of the 20th century was followed by the further discoveries and research of the first two decades of the 21st. This allows the story of Roman Exeter, from its beginnings until its ultimate demise, to be told with much greater confidence than at any time previously. The account which follows draws upon a vast amount of existing literature, all of which is listed in the section marked Further Reading at the end of the book.

It is my earnest hope that the book will be well received, both by the citizens of Exeter and by those beyond, interested in the story of a legionary garrison fortress that rapidly evolved into a Roman city on the very western edge of the Roman Empire.

John Pamment Salvatore
Isca Dumnoniorum
MMXXIII

General Notes

Copyright

Figures captioned (© RAMM) are from the archives of Exeter Archaeology and are copyright Royal Albert Memorial Museum & Art Gallery. Figures captioned (© ECC) are copyright of Exeter City Council. Figures 1; 26-27; 47; 98 and 106 were drawn by David Gould at the University of Exeter for the *Exeter: A Place in Time* project published in 2021 and are copyright of the authors (Rippon and Holbrook). Amendments to these figures for the purposes of this book have been undertaken by David Gould with the permission of the authors. All other figures carry copyright information within their individual captions.

Note on the orientation of the fortress and town gates

The Roman city of Exeter has its major street axes set out not in accordance with the cardinal points of the compass but approximately NE to SW and NW to SE. However, the city gates on all four sides of the town wall have, since time immemorial, been referred to respectively, as the North Gate, South Gate, East Gate and West Gate, and these names, still in everyday usage, are retained throughout this book. This 'constraint' does not apply to the gates of the earlier legionary fortress, which are described and shown with their correct geographical orientation (see Figure 1).

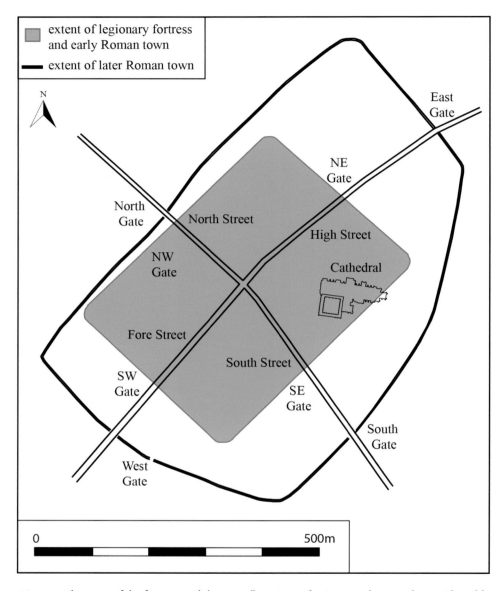

Figure 1. The gates of the fortress and the town (location and orientation). Drawn by David Gould

Note on the dating of archaeological material from Exeter and the published source material.

The archaeology of historic cities is usually described as being multi-period and deeply stratified. This is true of Exeter where the Roman levels in the city centre may be found below medieval and post-medieval deposits sometimes

3m or more below the modern ground surface. The archaeological deposits often comprise of successive layers of building debris and discarded rubbish. Cities which have been continuously occupied for hundreds or even thousands of years will accumulate sometimes significant depths of successive building remains on the same site. Due to the labour involved, and before the advent of earth moving machines, re-building would often see the demolition of the old followed by construction of the new without any large-scale clearance having taken place. Likewise, before relatively modern, and organised waste disposal, domestic rubbish was often discarded into the nearest redundant ditch, well, or pit. These rubbish deposits may contain material which can assist in the dating of the sequence when recovered during controlled archaeological excavation.

The dating of archaeological deposits from Exeter relies on two main sources, coin loss and pottery evidence. The reliability of coins and pottery as dating evidence varies considerably for the Roman occupation of Exeter - which broadly spans the period from the mid-first century AD until the last decades of the fourth. Pottery, particularly *terra sigillata* (or Samian ware as it is commonly known), is useful for establishing a chronology for the first few hundred years of Roman occupation. Samian is a high-quality, fine table ware which arrived in Britain in huge quantities following the Roman invasion of AD 43 and was in common usage by the Roman army and amongst the civilian Romano-British inhabitants in Romanised areas of Britain. The ware was mass produced in central and southern Gaul (modern France). A dish, bowl, or cup in Samian ware could be produced quickly by putting the initially wheel-thrown clay into a pre-prepared mould where the decoration had been applied in relief. The firing process produces the appearance of a high, shiny red gloss. Samian ware found in excavation at Exeter after nearly 2,000 years in the ground, can have the appearance of having been newly made (Figure 2).

It is often the case that a mould-maker's name will be stamped on the base of Samain vessels and sometimes those of individual potters. Furthermore, each mould-maker or potter would have had a working life. This allows pieces to be relatively closely dated, providing a chronology for other finds. For example, it will be self-evident that stamped Samian ware found damaged within the burnt destruction layers at Colchester, resulting from the sacking of the town during the revolt of Boudica in AD 60-61, must have been made before that date. The name stamp on the bottom of the Samian plate from Exeter shown in Figure 3 reads NESTORFE[C] (which may be read as *Nestor fe[cit]* = Nestor made this). A study of this mould-maker's stamp by Brenda Dickinson has produced an estimated period of production between *c.* AD 45-65. At Exeter, the ability to obtain close dating from Samian ware becomes more difficult in the final decades of the second century, whilst the supply to the city appears to

Figure 2. Roman Samian ware pottery. (© RAMM)

dry up in the early third century. Exeter is fortunate in that the Roman finds, including the pottery and coins recovered from all sources up until 1980, have been published by Neil Holbrook and Paul Bidwell as an Exeter Archaeological Report (1991, Vol. 4). It was supplemented the following year by a journal publication which took the study forward to cover the years 1980 to 1990.

Coins can offer good dating evidence given that they carry information about the emperor depicted, his current term of office, and when and where the coin was minted. Sometimes a known historical event is commemorated. For example, the coin of the Emperor Claudius seen in Figure 4 celebrates the capture of Britain (DE BRITANN inscribed on a triumphal arch) which means the coin must have been minted after the invasion of AD 43 In fact, the inscription around the head of Claudius tells the specialist that the coin was minted in Rome in AD 46-47.

The account of Roman Exeter which follows draws upon a vast amount of existing literature. All published source material, both ancient and modern, is listed in the section marked Further Reading at the end of the book.

Figure 3. A Samian ware plate base with maker's mould stamp
(NESTOR FE[C] = Nestor made this. (© RAMM)

Figure 4. A coin of the Emperor Claudius celebrating the conquest of Britain.
Left (obverse): the head of Claudius with his Imperial titles.
Right (reverse): victorious cavalry and infantry troops atop a triumphal arch inscribed
DE BRITANN. (© The Trustees of the British Museum)

Introduction

'.....no doubt the walls of the city are upon Roman foundations for the most part'.
William Stukeley 1724

Clearly visible and undisputed Roman masonry fabric of the town wall of Exeter survives both to the front and rear of its much rebuilt and repaired circuit (Figure 5). This gives physical testament of the Roman presence at the city, something which was recognised and commented upon in the reports of early antiquarians. One of them, Captain W.T.P. Shortt, moved to Exeter in 1832. He took advantage of a re-building programme which coincided with his arrival to study Roman pottery and coins from the several centuries of Roman occupation disturbed by the cellars of new shops and houses under construction. This research drew Shortt to the conclusion that Exeter owed its origin to the Roman military. He then went on to publish, by his own admission, an imaginary or *'supposed'* plan of the *'Roman camp of Isca'* based on the Greek historian Polybius' second century BC account of the layout of a tented camp.

By the late 19th and the first half of the 20th centuries, accounts of Roman Exeter had been published by R.N. Worth and V.E. Nash-Williams. The latter undertook some limited excavation from 1931until 1938 when, work ceased for the entirety of the war years, only to resume in 1945 with Lady Aileen Fox's investigations of the war-damaged areas of the city. Once life had resumed some semblance of normality, a conference on Romano-British *Civitas* (Regional) Capitals was held at the University of Leicester in December of 1963. A series of papers were delivered on what were then recent discoveries in several of the *Civitas* capitals undergoing post-war redevelopment. These papers included a

Figure 5. Distinctive Roman 'herring-bone' walling at the base of the rear of the Roman wall, Northernhay Gardens, Exeter. 2m scale. Photo: John Pamment Salvatore

report by Lady Fox on the post-War excavations at Exeter. At that time, Lady Fox had found no evidence for a Roman military presence at Exeter prior to the establishment of a civilian town in the mid-first century AD. At the same conference Graham Webster offered the view that there should nevertheless be a military origin for Exeter. Just one year later, Lady Fox did excavate a Roman ditch of mid-first century date at Exeter which she interpreted as the defences of a fort (Figure 6). However, the ditch was located beyond the town walls and although proving a Roman military presence just outside of the city, it could not be argued to be the direct precursor of the site chosen for the Roman civilian settlement. Thus, as we approached 1970 Exeter was known only as a Roman town dating from the mid-first century AD.

Figure 6. Lady Aileen Fox in a Roman military period ditch at the South Gate 1964. (© RAMM)

Chapter 1

No time to lose
(archaeological innovation and discovery at Exeter)

'Unlike the study of an ancient document, the study of a site by excavation is an unrepeatable experiment'.

Philip Barker 1993

The 'new' archaeologists

In late 1970 it was Lady Aileen Fox, then senior lecturer at the University of Exeter, and Patrick Boylan, director of the Royal Albert Memorial Museum, who came together to play a significant part in encouraging the formation and funding of an archaeological field unit for the city. The Exeter Museums Archaeological Field Unit (often referred to simply as: the Unit) was subsequently born in the following year of 1971. In its first full years of existence the Unit was dedicated exclusively to the excavation of proposed development sites within the administrative boundary of the city of Exeter (the extent of which included the medieval town of Topsham to the south). Exeter thus became one of the first local authorities to make such a provision for archaeology at a time when the centres of many historic towns in England, such as York and Winchester, were undergoing this same process of change. At Exeter, the initiative came not a moment too soon. Had the planned building programmes taken place without archaeological recording, then the massively damaging construction practices of the time would have removed the bulk of surviving archaeological deposits of all periods and along with them the precious information which they held; there would be no second chance.

It had been Aileen Fox's post-War work in the severely bomb-damaged city that had illustrated its rich archaeological potential, particularly for the Roman period. It was she who promoted the idea that the new unit should focus initially upon the opportunity for excavation that had arisen following the demolition of the redundant mid-19th century church of St Mary Major.

Figure 7. View of the 1972 excavation of the Roman military bathhouse from the Cathedral roof. Photo by Rob Turner (© RAMM). Note the car-park still in operation

The church, had for over a century, rather overshadowed the magnificent west front of the medieval Cathedral of St Peter. It was reported by Lady Fox that the respected historian, landscape archaeologist and one-time resident of Exeter, W.G. Hoskins had once mentioned that: *'There might be something worth excavating beneath St Mary Major Church'*. The church was intended to be replaced by an underground carpark, thus eliminating, once and for all, the car parking spaces which had been allowed to proliferate in the Cathedral Close, some just a few metres from the door of the west front (Figure 7). However, another major development site just behind the High Street,

Figure 8. John Collis at the Goldsmith Street site, Guildhall, 1971. (© RAMM)

and the medieval Guildhall, offered the rare opportunity for archaeological investigation over a large area in advance of the construction of the Guildhall Shopping Centre. In the end it was decided that both sites should proceed to full open-area excavation simultaneously. This proved to be a decision of monumental significance. When work began in earnest at the Guildhall and St Mary Major sites in 1971, John Collis, a lecturer in archaeology at the University of Exeter, was chosen to undertake the Goldsmith Street excavations at the Guildhall (Figure 8). Meanwhile, Michael Griffiths, the then assistant director of excavations at York, took charge of the St Mary Major operation. Griff, as he was known, was appointed as the Exeter Unit's first Museum Field Officer and shortly afterwards as its first director (Figure 9). The initial workforce of excavators, which in those days were known colloquially as 'diggers', were an eclectic mix of those who had worked before, either with Michael Griffiths or John Collis, on excavations in this country or abroad. They were supplemented by American exchange students, volunteers enlisted from the ranks of The Devon Archaeological Society, a small number of Exeter University archaeology students and a handful of untutored local recruits. A great many of those involved at the outset would never have encountered the multi-period urban archaeology that presented itself in the centre of Exeter.

Figure 9. Mike Griffiths excavating a Saxon 'charcoal burial' (which contained a gold ring) at the St Mary Major excavation, 1971. (© RAMM)

It was at this early stage in the formative life of the Unit that John Collis and Michael Griffiths brought in two archaeologists to assist them, both of whom were ideally suited to the task in hand – this being the successful and competent recording and interpretation of the archaeology at the two important sites which had been chosen for investigation ahead of destruction. Joining John Collis at the Guildhall was Christopher 'Chris' Henderson, whom, whilst still a young man, had developed a passion for the discipline of archaeology which saw him gain a vast level of excavation experience in the UK and on the Continent. When Collis departed Exeter in late 1971 to become a lecturer and later a professor of Prehistory at Sheffield, Chris Henderson at first supervised and then took over the running of the Goldsmith Street site (Figure 10). On the other side of the High Street at St Mary Major, Michael Griffiths remained in overall charge. His inspired choice of the recently graduated Exeter University law student Paul Bidwell (Figure 11) to conduct the day-to-day supervision and excavation of the site, was to lead ultimately to the publication of the Unit's first detailed and scholarly archaeological report, of which more later.

The two city-centre sites could hardly have been more different in the archaeological remains which were exposed and the challenging contexts in which their excavation took place. At St Mary Major the massive foundation walls of the Victorian church proved too great an obstacle to remove during the first season of excavation in 1971. Work thus proceeded within the stubbornly remaining below-ground-level foundations of the nave and the south aisle. Even then, and before archaeological levels could be reached, the excavators had to contend with a vast number of burials spanning a length of time extending from the immediate post-Roman period, through to and including the many hundreds of years during which the area had been the dedicated cemetery of the Cathedral. When burial in this location ceased in 1636 there was a hiatus until interment resumed in the 19th century following the construction

Figure 10. Chris Henderson on site in wet conditions at Goldsmith Street 1971.(© RAMM)

Figure 11. Paul Bidwell on site at St Mary Major in 1971 or 1972. (© RAMM)

of the St Mary Major church in 1867. All of the burials of whatever period required respectful recording and disinterment with subsequent re-burial in consecrated ground. When the site area was expanded towards the High Street in 1972, other features were encountered which caused further problems either in reaching the required depth for the recording of archaeological remains or preventing their exposure altogether. These disturbances included the crypt of a 13th or 14th century charnel-chapel and an extremely robust WWII concrete emergency water-tank which sealed off everything beneath it. A water-main, which ran across the site in 1971 and which necessitated the retention of a large baulk of unexcavated material in order to support it, was made redundant and removed.

Already, by the spring of 1972 it was known that the St. Mary Major site held the remains not only of a monumental stone-built Roman bathhouse of the mid-first century AD but also the basilica (central administrative building) of the city . These will be discussed in more detail in later chapters but the most important and fundamental fact arising from the excavation was that Exeter could be shown to have possessed a building the date, size and construction of which could only have been accomplished by a large and organised work-force. Only the Roman army could have supplied such numbers for the task at this early date.

Meanwhile, and of equal importance to the bathhouse discovery if not as visually impressive, were the initial results from the Goldsmith Street site at the Guildhall. John Collis, in the first season of 1971, had recognised, at the lowest archaeological levels, parallel trenches cut into the natural clay in all three of the separate excavation areas which had been opened up. These trenches were shown to be consistent with timber building foundations suspected to be Roman and to be of mid-first century AD date and thus contemporary with the bathhouse building at St. Mary Major. In his interim report on the 1971 excavations, Collis was able to state that: ‘*a military lay-out of Roman Exeter now seems a distinct possibility... the forthcoming 1972 excavations are certain to add appreciably to the picture......if we can obtain more of the plan of the early timber buildings we may be able to place their military origin beyond doubt*’. These words proved to be prophetic.

Unlike the St Mary Major site, where the magnitude of the 1971 discovery precluded all thought of future development (carpark or otherwise), work continued unabated at the Guildhall sites throughout the summer and winter months of 1972 and 1973. This was in order that construction of the proposed shopping centre could go ahead unhindered. Building upon the initial findings of 1971, Chris Henderson went on to the newly available area at Trichay Street to the west of Goldsmith Street. It is remarkable, given the levels of post-medieval disturbance, how much of the history of the two Guildhall sites of Goldsmith Street and Trichay Street was recovered. This was in no small measure due to the rigorous application of archaeological techniques pioneered first by John Collis and then by Chris Henderson; in some cases tailored specifically for the recording of urban archaeological deposits. The Roman deposits at the Guildhall sites had suffered terrible loss from the successive years of medieval and post-medieval activity which left sometimes only isolated areas of undisturbed archaeology. This may be seen in Figure 12 where the walls of a large fourth century Roman town house at Trichay Street survived only in a fragmented state.

All year-round excavation often resulted in less-than-optimal seasonal conditions when the lowest Roman levels were reached. The natural clay subsoil was sometimes baked hard by the sun or conversely, presented a quagmire after heavy rain. Despite this, and with a relatively inexperienced digging crew, Chris Henderson took exceptional pains to extract the maximum amount of information from the excavations. Where exposed, all of the Roman timber building trenches were meticulously excavated and planned at different stages in the process with the result that subtle archaeological observations could be made. For example, the presence of wooden posts or stakes within the trenches could be identified

Figure 12. The heavily disturbed and fragmented walls of a Late Roman town house at the Guildhall site of Trichay Street 1972. 2m scales. (© RAMM)

by their archaeological signal - the circular discolouration created by natural process of soil movement when the physical remains of the wood has long since gone. Had the trench fills been emptied without this painstaking step then somewhat fewer of the post locations would have been spotted and the process of building construction not necessarily fully understood.

Reaping the benefits

The attention to detailed best practice had its reward, exemplified by the fact that the building trenches at the Guildhall sites, suspected to be of Roman military origin, could be demonstrated archaeologically to have been of a type of construction known as post-trench (sometimes called post-in-trench). This was a commonplace timber building method employed by the Roman army at military establishments across the breadth of Roman controlled north-western Europe by the first century AD. The technique involved the digging of trenches for the outer walls of the building into which were placed upright wooden posts in post-holes (Figure 13). The trenches were then backfilled around the posts creating a structurally sound earthfast framework. Wattle and daub wall sections were then added between the uniformly spaced main uprights with the aid of smaller stakes

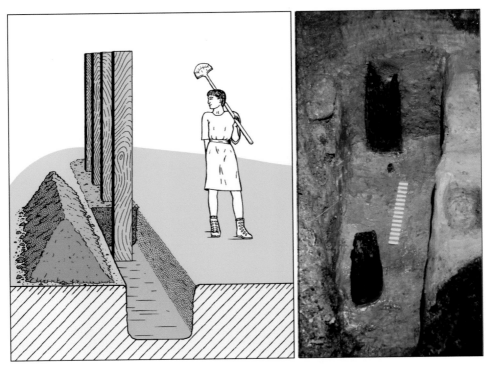

Figure 13. Left: the Roman post-trench building technique drawn by J.R.L. Thorpe.
Right: a Roman post-trench with surviving waterlogged posts - 30cm scale. (© RAMM)

interspersed between the gaps. Very occasionally the lower sections of the upright wooden posts survived in waterlogged conditions (Figure 13). The walls once dried could be rendered and plastered. Internal walls and partitions could be created using the same method as the outer load-bearing walls, but with foundation trenches appreciably shallower. Eventually, sufficient numbers of post-trenches at the Goldsmith Street and Trichay Street sites had been recorded on the master plan which enabled them to be identified as Roman army barracks. Furthermore, their size, design and ordered arrangement, as part of a group of six paired buildings, led to the conclusion by early 1973, that these were barracks constructed for elite troops of the Roman army – in this instance those of a Roman legionary cohort. The legionary accommodation is discussed in further detail in Chapter 3.

The Roman barracks at the bottom of the archaeological sequence at the Guildhall sites were only one part of the overall site history. The recording of all periods represented benefitted from the introduction by Chris Henderson of the latest archaeological techniques of the day, including the deployment of the so-called Harris Matrix. The eponymous matrix took its name from Ed Harris who is credited with developing and codifying its use in 1973. At its simplest, the matrix provided the best visual method of recording urban archaeological sequences. Every deposit between the undisturbed natural ground at the base and the modern ground level at the top was shown on the paper 'flow chart' in its correct stratigraphic location following excavation. When the dating evidence from pottery or coins is later analysed in relation to this relative chronology then the archaeological story of the site can be extracted. The Exeter timeline suggests that Henderson was already using similar principles to those developed by Harris at least one year earlier in 1972.

Where archaeological deposits do not survive sufficiently in the horizontal plane then a 'story' may still be told by diligent examination of any on-site vertical exposure (i.e., a section). For example, the removal of a cellar wall may reveal behind it a slice through the entire archaeological sequence from top to bottom. Henderson seized upon opportunities of this nature which occurred on the Goldsmith and Trichay Street sites and committed many hours to the subsequent exhaustive 'interrogation' of the section until all of the individual layers or features had been identified. Following this, a detailed drawing was made. Such an assiduous approach proved to be invaluable for interpretation purposes, engendering, as it did, on-site debate which could never be as incisive if deferred to later post-excavation analysis of the section drawings alone. Figure 14 shows a simple section through late Roman deposits at the Goldsmith Street site. Several Roman layers have been exposed including one floor which has been laid on a mortar bed above a pitched stone base. Above the floor is a demolition deposit which includes building stone and at least

Figure 14. Section through Late Roman archaeological deposits at Goldsmith Street. At the base is the light-coloured natural clay of the Roman ground surface. Above this are the pitched stones of a Roman floor foundation followed by occupation deposits; all then sealed by demolition layers. 1m scale. (© RAMM)

one sherd of what appears to be the rim of a storage jar. The 'art' of section interpretation had been so successfully instilled into those working at the Guildhall sites that a few years later, in 1975, the traces of Roman timber houses were identified solely by this method at a building site in Mary Arches Street, where the archaeological deposits were visible only for a relatively short period of time in the sides of modern foundation trenches which were awaiting poured concrete.

Halcyon days

The opening up of large-scale excavation sites by a locally based professional archaeological unit in the early years of the 1970s, captured the imagination of the citizens of Exeter who flocked to view areas of the city which had remained buried for the best part of two thousand years. By far the greater numbers were attracted to the St Mary Major site in the Cathedral Close where, separated from 'the dig' only by a chestnut-paling fence, they could see at close quarters the exposed and spectacular inner workings of a Roman bathhouse. Such was the interest, that an information board was erected upon which it was proclaimed that the remains: *belonged to one of the largest and best-preserved Roman baths in Britain*. The most frequently posed question from those looking on was: *what have you found?* (Figure 15). The excavations literally became headline news with periodic updates on their progress appearing on the front pages of the local newspaper the *Exeter Express and Echo* (Figure 16).

Figure 15. The public look on whilst excavation takes place in front of the
Cathedral's West Front. (© RAMM)

It was not only the citizens of Exeter who were caught up in the excitement generated by the sight of teams of archaeologists operating on two major sites within a few minutes walking distance of each other. A product of the camaraderie that formed within the ranks of those working for the Unit was the desire of all to participate in putting forward interpretive ideas through on-site debate at the trench edge, in the pub, or back at the 'dig house'. In its first years many of the Unit's diggers, site supervisors and the assistant directors lived together in shared houses which further promoted this sense of team spirit (Figure 17). Whilst much serious work was going on at the site, the 'diggers' themselves (both male and female and often in their 20s) took on the fashions of the day,

Figure 16. Front page of the Exeter Express and
Echo (9th July 1971)

Figure 17. Paul Bidwell (back row, centre) and the St Mary Major digging crew 1972.
Photo by Rob Turner. (© RAMM)

sometimes adopting the outward appearance of a 70s rock band (Figure 18). Life-long friendships were made, or future collaborative relationships were created. Of those who worked for the Unit in the 1970s it might be suspected that the majority would agree with the view that the decade was one of a golden period for the archaeology of the city.

The Legacy

It is beyond the scope of this book to attempt anything other than touch briefly upon the enormous benefits accrued to the city of Exeter following the creation of an Archaeological Field Unit. By 1972 Chris Henderson had already been appointed as one of two deputy directors, the other post going to Paul Bidwell. Henderson was subsequently offered the post of Director in 1975 when the incumbent Michael Griffiths departed to take a curatorial role in Yorkshire. Thus began a 25-year period in which Henderson fashioned and nurtured a first-class excavation unit which oversaw astonishing levels of recording in the city and beyond. He did this – not just through promoting and maintaining the highest levels of on-site archaeological practice, but also by participating himself, or supporting others, in the fields of documentary research and historic building recording. In fact, Henderson's commitment to building recording and documentary research as part of the whole integrated archaeological

Figure 18. Unit diggers from the Guildhall sites at the medieval Exe Bridge in 1974.
Photo by Nigel Cheffers-Heard. (© RAMM)

process was ground-breaking in the early 70s and was undertaken in few other places at that time. Paul Bidwell continued in the role of Deputy Director following Henderson's appointment and devoted himself to the writing up of the military bathhouse and basilica. This he completed and published in 1979 before leaving the Unit in the year afterwards for Hadrian's Wall.

A significant new addition to the ranks of the Unit came with the arrival of Neil Holbrook in 1986 as an Assistant Field Archaeologist. Holbrook had a keen interest in the Roman period and in particular the Roman pottery supply to the fortress and the later town. In his three years at the Unit he collaborated with Paul Bidwell in producing a major report on the Roman finds from Exeter. The volume, published in 1991, was the fourth in the Exeter Archaeological Reports series and dealt primarily with the pottery finds made by the Unit during those intense years of archaeological investigation which took place, both within and just outside the town walls between 1971-1979.

A sea-change in archaeological practice in England occurred in 1990 when archaeological investigation on development sites was brought into the Government's planning system. The onus was put on the developers to pay for the costs of archaeological investigation, analysis, and publication if their proposals were otherwise to result in the loss of significant archaeological remains without record. Under Chris Henderson's guidance the Unit soon adapted to this new way of working and in 1995 it was re-branded as Exeter Archaeology. Still known as The Unit, it began operations as a self-funded service under the auspices of Exeter City Council, who provided a business premises within the city. Throughout the quarter of a century during which Chris Henderson had administered the organisation, he continued to work on numerous projects, including but not exclusively, the study of the layout of the legionary fortress, the design of its bathhouse and the evolution of the city's Roman South Gate, before his untimely death in 2001 robbed the city and the wider archaeological community of future scholarly reports. Of the three areas of study named above, two were published whilst he was still alive and one, the Roman South Gate, posthumously – all three feature in this book.

Subsequent directors of Exeter Archaeology following on from Chris Henderson were Peter Weddell and then Tim Gent. Exeter Archaeology ceased operations in 2011 after experiencing significant financial difficulties, not least as a result of the economic downturn of 2008, but not before excavating some remarkable new Roman sites in and around the city. These included a major new discovery at the former St Loye's College on Topsham Road (some 2.2 km south-east of the city), and the Unit's last major open area excavation site within the walls at the Princesshay shopping centre redevelopment between 2005 and 2006.

Chapter 2

The Roman army arrives at Exeter

'...he (Claudius) disarmed the Britons and handed them over to Plautius, whom he authorised to subjugate the remaining areas'.
Dio Cassius (second to third century AD)

The Roman army in the South-West

It has long been established that the four Roman legions which invaded Britain at the behest of the Emperor Claudius in AD 43, were the Twentieth *Valeria*, the Ninth *Hispana,* the Fourteenth *Gemina,* and the Second *Augusta.* Of these four, it is the Second Augustan Legion (*Legio II Augusta*) which is of particular interest for our purposes as this legion's Legate (senior officer), when it alighted on these shores, was Titus Flavius Vespasianus, who later, in AD 69, became the Emperor Vespasian. Suetonius, a Roman historian of the second century AD, wrote an account of the lives of twelve Caesars (Emperors) one of whom was Vespasian. Suetonius tells us that Vespasian, as commander of the Second Augustan Legion, captured the Island of *Vectis* (the Isle of Wight). This puts the legion's area of campaign in the south of Britain but not necessarily confined to the south coast; they may have been campaigning at the outset across a wide area west of London. Eberhard Sauer has argued that a timber-built fortress discovered at Alchester in Oxfordshire (known by dendrochronological tree-ring dating to have been constructed by AD 44/45 at the latest), may have been an early campaign base for Vespasian following the invasion. Vespasian had the 5,000 legionary troops of the Second Augustan at his disposal, plus an equal force of auxiliaries. These forces may have been brought together in battle groups to engage with any organised resistance or simply sent into new territory in an open display of strength. The sight of a full legion arriving on the march may well have been enough to deter any thoughts of opposition.

In addition to the capture of the Isle of Wight, Suetonius tells us that Vespasian reduced to submission two unnamed powerful war-like tribes and overcame twenty *oppida* (towns or hillforts). Can we accept these claims and figures literally and uncritically? Suetonius was, after all, writing eighty years or so after the events in question. Could the Durotriges, the Iron Age tribe whose territory included Dorset, parts of Wiltshire and southern parts of Somerset, be one of the two war-like tribes mentioned by Suetonius, and were some of the twenty hillforts taken by Vespasian theirs? In the post-WWII period some scholars thought that Durotrigian resistance to Rome was likely, bringing with it continuous conflict. Countering this argument, archaeologists and researchers from Bournemouth University conducted a renewed period of archaeological fieldwork across the hillforts of Dorset and published their findings between 2017 and 2020. They found no evidence that any of the hillforts of Dorset were militarily active during the first century AD when the Second Augustan Legion was occupying and moving through the area. Settlement instead apparently comprised of communities in lightly enclosed farmsteads. Therefore, could the subjugation of at least some of those twenty *oppida* credited to Vespasian have been hillforts which were completely abandoned at the time of the invasion or only very lightly occupied? Furthermore, it was long thought by archaeologists that one of the *oppida* captured must have been the massive hillfort of Maiden Castle near Dorchester. Even this is now in doubt; or rather, the picture which the famous archaeologist Sir Mortimer Wheeler presented does not now stand up to scrutiny. Wheeler excavated what he claimed was a 'war cemetery', in which the Iron Age occupants and defenders of Maiden Castle were hurriedly buried following their slaughter by Vespasian's forces. Archaeological work and re-analysis of the skeletal remains has demonstrated that none of those burials within the cemetery can convincingly be shown to have died in defence of the hillfort. Only a few of the 52 burials excavated by Wheeler had what might be described as injuries inflicted by weapons. The majority had been carefully buried with grave goods including personal ornaments, in the period between the mid-first century BC and the late-first century AD, within a well-established burial ground. Funerary rituals such as this do not suggest hastily dug graves following a single battle, but a cemetery that was used over an extended period of time.

Leaving aside the question of the level of conflict which the Roman presence in Durotrigian territory may or may not have generated, we do know that a legionary base was constructed at Lake Farm near Wimborne in Dorset, and this in all probability before AD 50 (Figure 19). It is plausible that Lake Farm was intended as the Second Augustan Legion's campaign base prior to the

Figure 19. Aerial reconstruction of Lake Farm fortress in Dorset based upon geophysical survey results. (© David John and Bournemouth University)

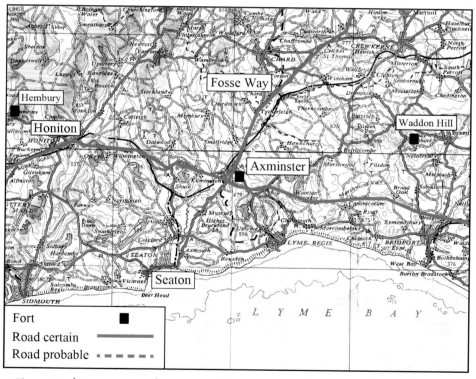

Figure 20. The Fosse Way and Roman roads in Somerset and East Devon (after Toller 2014). Redrawn by David Gould

push further westwards into the far south-western peninsula of Britain. Those lands, broadly speaking the Devon and Cornwall of today, were inhabited by peoples who are generally known as the Dumnonii. It is unclear whether there was what we would consider a recognisably firm border between the Dumnonii and the Durotriges to the east. Definitive borders and name classifications are convenient for our descriptive purposes but are likely to have been observed differently by those living at the time. Neil Holbrook has rightly cautioned that: *we should not uncritically assume that the Dumnonii necessarily possessed a unified identity that stretched back into the pre-Roman Iron Age or extended over the whole of the Peninsula.*

At some stage, believed to be around AD 47, the construction of the road known as the Fosse Way commenced. The Fosse Way, in its first iteration, joined together several long sections of road to complete a course that ran all the way from Lincoln in the north to Ilchester in the south, onwards to Axminster and with a probable continuation to Seaton (Figure 20). A termination at Seaton suggests that in the mid-first century it may have been possible to land supplies at the sheltered inlet at the mouth of the River Axe before later silting made this impossible. The Second Augustan Legion was probably involved in the construction of the Fosse Way within the modern counties of Somerset and Devon. If so, the areas either side of the River Axe in Devon and the River Parrett in Somerset, must have been sufficiently secured for the Fosse Way roadbuilding programme to have proceeded presumably unhindered. The manpower needed for the task of roadbuilding across such vast distances may have played a part, together with any wider political considerations, in a delay in making the incisive penetrating advance further westward. That is not to say that diplomatic missions into the far South-West or seaborne reconnaissance along the coasts of Devon and Cornwall had not taken place before any major landward incursion. Evidence of one such probing event on the border of Devon and Cornwall may exist. A coin hoard of the Emperor Claudius (AD 41-54) from Roborough, on the east bank of the River Tavy just north of Plymouth, was recovered in 1989. The coins were studied by Norman Shiel who concluded that these Claudian issues (and one of Gaius - Caligula) of no later than AD 41-42, favour a date of deposition prior to the foundation of the legionary fortress at Exeter around AD 55 (see below). They were suggested by Neil Holbrook to have been hidden for later retrieval by an advance military reconnaissance or raiding party, whilst the main bulk of the army was still in Dorset.

Ultimately, the Roman army would have driven forward to complete the conquest of the South-West, which would always have been the intention when the time, the seasonal weather conditions, and the readiness of the campaign force were all considered to be favourable, and intelligence gathering had been completed. The time-frame for this advance and the completion of the task set by the Emperor Claudius, at least in the far South-West, would appear therefore to be between *c.* AD 47 and *c.* AD 55. This is not to say that the campaign took up to eight years; it may have been far shorter but dating evidence for the event is next to non-existent. What we can say with some confidence is that Vespasian is believed to have returned to Rome by this time and that the Second Augustan Legion would have had a new commander, whose name is unknown to us, as it pushed westwards. A military road would have been constructed extending from the Fosse Way at Axminster to Exeter and beyond to facilitate the advance. Hard evidence of the campaign on the ground in the South-West is difficult to come by. Temporary marching camps, often short-lived and occupied by rows of tents rather than buildings, leave little trace other than their ditched defences which become infilled over the course of the millennia and thus largely invisible to the naked eye. A complex of marching camps or seasonal bases of different sizes, and all undated, were photographed from the air and commented upon in detail by the former Devon County Council Principal Archaeologist Frances Griffith in 1984, at North Tawton on the east bank of the River Taw about 26km west of Exeter. The precise number of camps is unclear, but two of the marching camps appear from their stratigraphic relationship to belong to successive use of the same site at different times.

Of particular interest at North Tawton are what appear to be the double-ditched defences of a very large camp. Chris Smart of Exeter University has employed non-intrusive geo-physical prospection techniques to add appreciably to what was previously known. He is now able to propose that the defended area of the large camp may have encompassed some 12.6ha, which could easily accommodate the tents of a legion and those of its auxiliary cohorts, or some other large concentration of troops which might comprise a battle group on campaign. Temporary marching or campaign camps of this size are commonly termed vexillation camps or bases in order to distinguish them from permanent fortresses. The defences of similar sized large camps to that at North Tawton have now been detected at another site in Devon at Rashleigh, Eggesford, and at Trerank, Roche which is well down into Cornwall (Figure 21).

Legionaries on campaign will have looked like those depicted in Figure 22. Here we see an 8-man tent-group (*contubernium*) breaking camp with the legionary at the front ready for the march and already carrying everything which might be required for fighting or encamping whilst on campaign. Thus, in addition to his sword, javelin, dagger, helmet and shield (in its protective covering) the legionary was expected to carry wooden stakes and entrenching tools, as

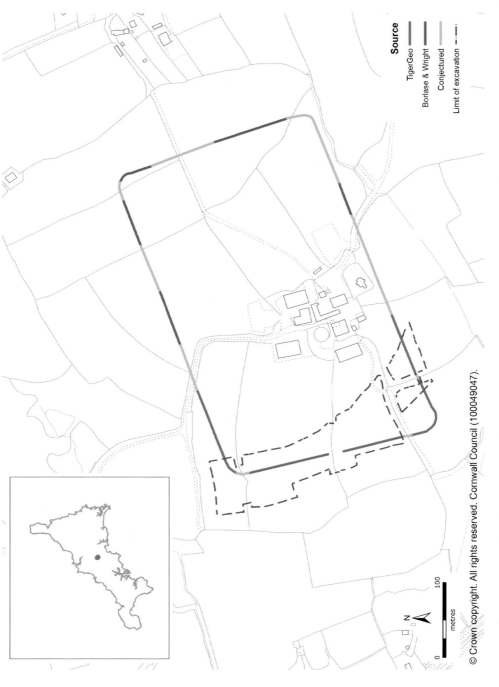

Figure 21. The part-excavated and part-plotted defences of a large marching camp at Trerank, Cornwall. (© Sean Taylor CAU, Cornwall Council)

Figure 22. Imaginative drawing of an eight-man legionary tent group (*contubernium*) breaking camp. (© akg-images/Peter Connolly)

well as his rations, cooking utensils and drinking water. Together, the weight of his *impedimenta* might amount to some 45kg. Given the amount of gear which they had to carry with them the legionaries were nicknamed 'Marius' Mules', after the Republican general, Gaius Marius, who cut down the size of baggage trains moving with the legions, thus requiring more of the campaign equipment to be distributed amongst the men. Their armour, either chain mail, scale, or segmented, was worn on the body whilst marching. That most often seen in any first century representation of a legionary is a type known as *lorica segmentata*. The articulation of the separate plates allowed free movement of the arms and shoulders (Figure 23). Heavy weaponry, such as a ballista (a type of mounted crossbow for throwing bolts), could be carried by mules along with the heavy goat-skin tents. The legionaries were responsible for their own kit which was probably supplied on enlistment with payment docked from their salary over time. On retirement the kit could be sold back to the army to be re-issued.

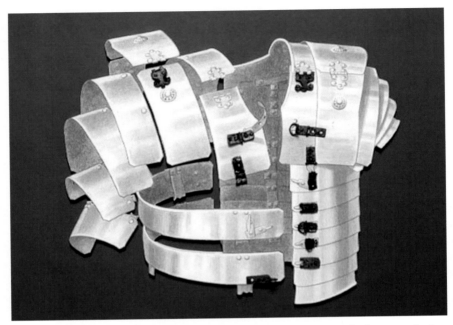

Figure 23. Illustration depicting the segmented armour (*lorica segmentata*) of a Roman legionary.
(© RAMM)

Exeter chosen as the site for a legionary fortress

That it was the Second Augustan Legion which built and occupied the fortress at Exeter now seems beyond doubt for reasons given in the next chapter. The date of *c.* AD 55 for its foundation is based upon the known pottery and coin evidence from the earliest excavated levels, with the caveat that *c.* AD 55-60 would cover most of the possibilities. This would put the foundation of the fortress early in the years of the Emperor Nero (AD 54-68). Auxiliary forts were built to the east of the fortress at about the same time (see Figure 20). The fort at Woodbury, Axminster was constructed *c.* AD 55-60 at the junction of the Fosse Way and the Dorchester to Exeter road. The forts at Waddon Hill in Dorset and Hembury in Devon appear at about the same time. The Hembury 'fort' comprises of Roman military buildings placed within the defences of an abandoned Iron Age hillfort. The site may have been associated with the exploitation of iron ore from the Blackdown Hills used for nails in the construction of timber buildings for the Exeter fortress.

An historical context for the establishment of the fortress is provided by the governorship of Didius Gallus in AD 52-57. During his time there may have been a general re-organisation of the western frontiers of the new province. This could be seen as being intended to complete the conquest of Britain (the task with which the first governor of the province, Aulus Plautius had been charged according to the Roman historian Dio Cassius). That Exeter had already been selected for what was intended to be the base for a legionary presence in South-West Britain is highly likely. The site, which had been picked out by the Roman military strategists, possessed several favourable topographical advantages. Thus, the legionary fortress was sited on the east side of the River Exe upon a naturally defended spur and with only one level approach from the east. The spur overlooked the river at a point where a change in geological formation resulted in the strong and constrained single-channel flow of the river becoming diffused into a series of channels. This phenomenon (known as anabranching) would have allowed a fordable crossing of the river in Roman times. The siting of the fortress above this crossing point suggests that this was the optimum location for the legionary base. Furthermore, the fortress was sited upriver of the then highest tidal reach which would place it, and the crossing point, above mud-sided, twice-daily inundated channels at a time when it is assumed that any other viable crossing point must have been much further inland. Essentially, the placement of the fortress was determined by the local geology, the resultant general topography and form of the fluvial regime, together with its strategic dimension.

A clear military advantage stemming from the fortress location was that any hostile force would not have the ability to cross the River Exe either undetected or unopposed. Conversely, a Roman legion, from its Exeter base, could control the river crossing and would have the capacity to move at speed in the opposite direction to quell unrest if the need arose. A consequence of the Exeter location was that the fortress could not be supplied directly by sea or even by river-barge. However, this was seemingly of lesser importance than its strategic location and the deficit, if it could be called such, was overcome in an efficient and pragmatic way by the creation of supporting infrastructure. In fact, there is every reason to believe that when the legion began work on the construction of the fortress, there was already a road connecting it to a facility further down the river at the head of the Exe estuary at Topsham where supplies could be unloaded and transported further inland on the purpose-built road (see Chapter 5 for further discussion of this arrangement).

Chapter 3

The Legionary Fortress
(and its stone-built bathhouse)

"As far as choice of ground is concerned, sites which are lifted gently from a field to a height have first place.....The Porta Praetoria (front gate) should always face the enemy'. Moreover, a camp will have a river or spring on some side'.
de munitionibus castrorum (Pseudo-Hyginus, late first-early second century AD)

The setting out of the fortress (the Henderson 'blueprint')

It might seem that the choice of Exeter had been made in accordance with a military handbook (known to the Romans as *vade mecum*), which advanced the same considerations as those outlined in a Roman treatise on military surveying (see quote above). That is to say, the ideal camp should have a river to one side, should have its main front gate facing the enemy, and should slope upwards towards high ground. The Exeter fortress could claim all three of these specifications, although it is a moot point whether the peoples inhabiting the lands west of Exeter could ever have been considered an enemy in the truest sense of the word. Having chosen the site, the first task in the creation of the fortress would have been the clearance of the land required, in this case some 19.6 ha. In relation to the modern city this equates to a rectangular area well within the later Roman town walls (see Figure 24). Woodland and scrub would have been removed from the selected area along with any contemporary native habitations of which there may have been very few. Henrietta Quinnell has commented that much of Devon would have seen a landscape of patches of woodland with areas laid out in fields and with a scatter of houses often in pairs, whilst the closest Iron Age hillforts to Exeter for which we have data do not appear to have been actively in use at the time of the Roman arrival.

Figure 24. Aerial photo of Exeter showing the approximate line of the fortress defences in blue and the later town wall circuit in red. (© Frances Griffith Devon County Council). Additions by David Gould

Once the initial ground preparation had taken place the fortress would have been constructed according to a pre-ordained set of guidelines. The legionary surveyors (*agrimensores*) would first have established the area of the fortress which was to be enclosed by the defences. Following this, the street alignments and the various different-sized plots for the barracks and other buildings

Figure 25. An artist's impression of military surveyors (*agrimensores*) at work (author's collection)

obligatory for a legionary fortress would have been marked out. Whilst no two forts or fortresses will be the same in every detail, nearly all of those in Britain of mid-to-late first century AD date shared certain common characteristics. These included a rectangular playing card shape with a gate in each of the four sides, four corner towers and evenly spaced interval towers along every side. The surveyors used an instrument called a *groma* for laying out right angles (see Figure 25). Two major streets of the fortress would have intersected at right angles to one another, in front of the plot chosen for the headquarters building (*principia*). One of these streets, the *via principalis,* ran crossways and connected two opposing gates in the defences. The other street, known as the *via praetoria,* ran from the *principia* to the main gate (*porta praetoria*). This produces the typical T-shaped plan of the fortress interior. Figure 26 illustrates this and gives the Latin terms which the Roman surveyors would have employed when laying out the fortress. Following Roman practice, left and right are taken from the position of an observer looking outwards towards the main gate at the front of the fort from the headquarters building (the *principia*). The gate to the right was known as the *porta principalis dextra* and the gate to the left, the *porta principalis sinistra.* On a conventional and stylised modern plan of the fortress (such as Figure 26) we are looking in the opposite direction to the Romans. As a result, their left-hand gate (*sinistra*) appears on the right-side of our plan and, vice versa, their right-hand gate (*dextra*), is shown on the left. The lesser road running from the

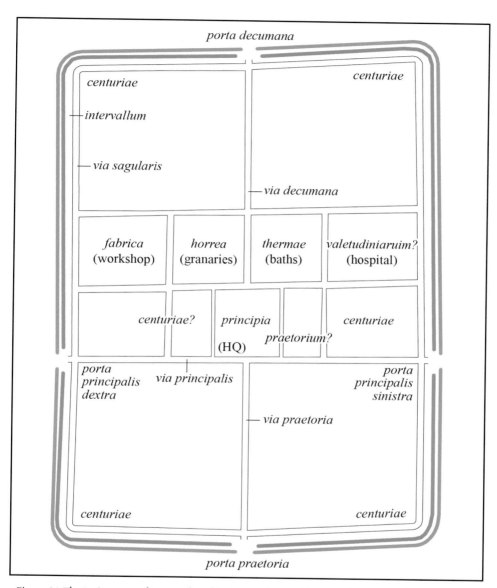

porta decumana

centuriae

centuriae

intervallum

via sagularis

via decumana

| fabrica (workshop) | horrea (granaries) | thermae (baths) | valetudiniaruim? (hospital) |

centuriae?

principia (HQ)

praetorium?

centuriae

porta principalis dextra

via principalis

porta principalis sinistra

via praetoria

centuriae

centuriae

porta praetoria

Figure 26. The Latin terminology employed for Roman fort and fortress plans. Drawn by David Gould

rear of the headquarters building to the rear gate (*porta decumana*) was known as the *via decumana*.

In addition to the evidence for the legionary barracks and a military bathhouse first identified in the very early 1970s, the rampart and ditch defences of the fortress began to appear in various excavations carried out during the same decade and the one following. As a result, it became possible for the

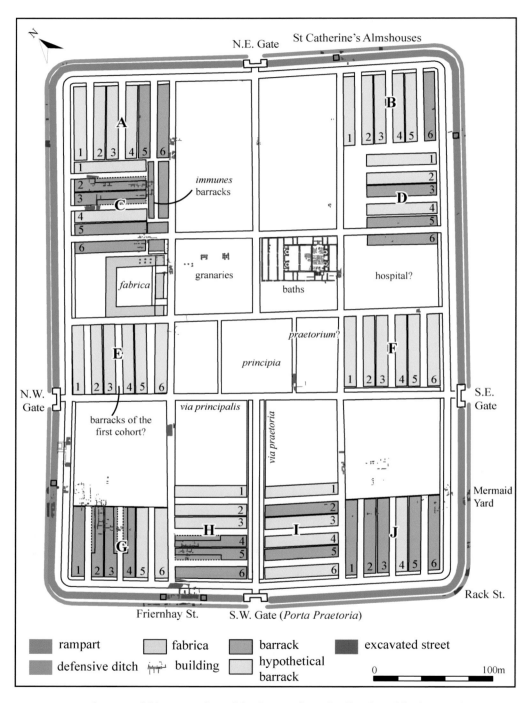

Figure 27. The revised 'blueprint plan' of the fortress (by Bidwell and Gould) after Henderson. Scale 1:2500. Drawn by David Gould. Cohort blocks are marked A-J

Exeter Archaeological Unit Director Chris Henderson to devote his energies to a detailed study of the layout of the fortress. Ultimately, he was able to demonstrate that the main gate faced towards the river rather than away from it as had been assumed when the fortress was first identified. He did this by creating on paper a hypothetical reconstruction of the fortress plan; effectively a 'blueprint' as it might have appeared in a Roman military instruction manual. Published in 1989, Henderson's highly technical paper argues a plan taking the known internal T-shape of a Roman fort as its starting point (see above) but then applying established rules of proportion and various design modules based upon multiples of one Roman foot (*pes Monetalis*), which is approximately 30cm. This plan, with later revisions by Bidwell and Gould in 2021 (see Figure 27), is the one which is still in use to predict the location of fortress buildings or defences where development is proposed in the centre of Exeter. The extent of the defensive circuit and the layout of the internal street system were the key elements to the understanding of this plan. Once sufficient sightings of these had taken place, Henderson was able to apply known Roman metrology to arrive at his blueprint. In the pages which follow it is possible to chart this journey.

The fortress defences

Timber-built Roman forts or fortresses intended for lengthy occupation will almost always have been provided with defences on all four sides and Exeter was no exception. These defences usually comprised of an earth rampart surmounted by a wooden palisade and fronted by a defensive ditch or ditches. The fortress ditch at Exeter was first encountered at Rack Street in 1974 and 1978 and again in 1978 at Mermaid Yard (see Figure 27 for locations). Where sectioned at Mermaid Yard, the ditch had a sharp V-shaped profile with a cleaning or drainage slot in the bottom. It was about 2.5m wide and 2m deep (Figure 28). A second parallel ditch with an asymmetrical profile was found a little further out. Initially, it was thought that both ditches were part of a double-ditch system protecting the fortress, but it later transpired that the outer ditch was part of the defences of the early town - it is discussed later. It was fortuitous that the fortress ditch, where exposed at Rack Street, was seen to be curving in a manner that matched the rounded-corner, 'playing-card', frequently seen in aerial photographs of Roman forts when showing as cropmarks or earthworks (see Figure 29). It unmistakably pointed to this excavation having hit upon the south-eastern corner of the defensive circuit (Figure 30). The consequence of this was that two sides of the fortress defences, those on the south-east and south-western sides, could tentatively be placed, and their alignments extrapolated.

Figure 28. The V-shaped defensive ditch of the legionary fortress exposed in section at Mermaid Yard, 1978. 2m scale. (© RAMM)

Figure 29. Aerial view of the crop marks and features marking two successive auxiliary forts at Cullompton, Devon. The rounded corners of the smaller inner fort's double-ditch defences and its gateway entrances are clearly seen. Photo by F.M. Griffith. (© Devon County Council)

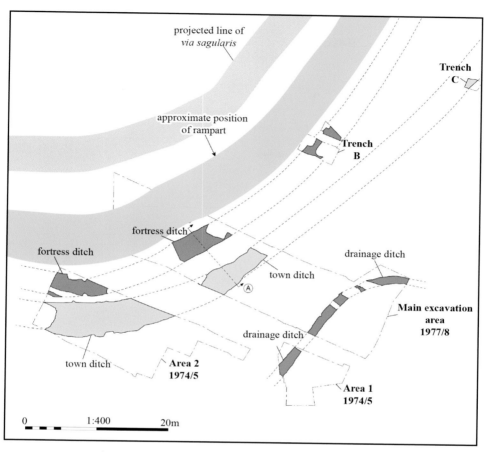

Figure 30. Plan of the legionary and later town defences at Rack Street, 1974-78.
Drawn by David Gould. (© Cotswold Archaeology)

At Mermaid Yard there was the first sighting at Exeter of the fortress rampart. Originally several metres in height, it survived as a 90cm high and 6m wide construction of redeposited clay-earth. Clay blocks at the front of the rampart suggest that it was turf faced and was separated from the inner edge of the ditch by a berm (walkway) about 1m wide; the berm allowed for access to the front of the rampart for repair purposes.

Seven years after the Rack Street and Mermaid Yard observations, confirmation of the rampart and ditch defence on the south-western side of the fortress facing the River Exe came in spectacular fashion at the Friernhay Street excavation of 1981 (see Figure 27 for location). Investigated in advance of a housing development, the site was the largest ever to have been undertaken on the line of the fortress defences. Here, a long stretch (up to 48m in length) of the ditch, rampart, *intervallum* and *via sagularis* were exposed (Figure 31).

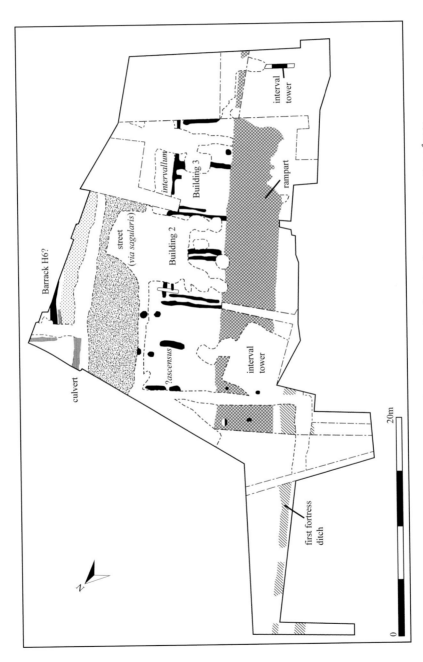

Figure 31. Plan of the fortress features exposed at the Friernhay Street excavation of 1981. Redrawn by David Gould. (© RAMM)

The *intervallum,* is the area between the rampart and the *via sagularis* which is the street which runs around the inside of the fortress, and which allows quick access to the rampart. The V-shaped fortress ditch was found with the same dimensions as those recorded at Mermaid Yard. The rampart was detected with a width of 4.6m and a surviving height of about 1m. The body of the rampart consisted of mixed compacted clays, almost certainly derived from the digging of the fortress ditch, and it was held front and rear between revetment cheeks of turf and fine clay. Timber strapping would have served to bind the structure together. When the rampart material was excavated down to the Roman ground surface it was found that it had been seated upon parallel logs and branches which would have provided stability to the base (Figure 32).

Behind the rampart and situated on the *intervallum* were a number of buildings which were probably associated with food preparation; at a later date they were replaced by buildings which held ovens. These buildings, where cooking presented a fire risk, were separated from the barracks beyond by the perimeter street (the *via sagularis*). A culvert allowed water to run parallel to the street. The supply was later enclosed within wooden water pipes. Several lengths of a narrow pipe were joined together by iron collars. The pipe and collar materials had decayed in such a way as to leave an unmistakeable archaeological 'footprint' of their presence.

Figure 32. Evidence of the log corduroy at the base of the legionary rampart at Friernhay Street. 2m scale. (© RAMM)

The Friernhay Street excavation provided evidence of exceptional importance. Located at the base of the rampart and sealed by the log corduroy were the enormous post-pits which had once held the massive timber posts (about 25cm in girth), of two observation interval towers spaced about 30m apart (Figure 33). The archaeological sequence clearly demonstrated that the timber towers had first been erected and then the rampart constructed around their supporting posts thus leaving the observation platform at some height above the top of the rampart. Further evidence of the timber foundations of a stairway (*ascensus*) was found behind the northernmost tower. Interval and corner towers are well known features common to both Roman forts and fortresses.

With the line of the defences established on two sides by 1981, the other two sides, those on the north-west and north-east, became known by the mid-1980s. The fortress ditch on the north-west side was seen in an archaeological trench at Paul Street in 1982, whilst the north-eastern corner of the defences was glimpsed in a road surface enhancement scheme at Upper Paul Street just beside the museum in 1986. By remarkable coincidence the run of kerbstones, which were being re-laid as part of the scheme, were found to match the curvature of the outer lip of the ditch which was exposed below (Figure 34). Significant evidence relating to the defences then arrived with the excavation in 1987 at the St. Catherine's Alms Houses site on the north-east defences (Figure 27 for location). Here, the turf stack at the front of the rampart could

Figure 33. Interval tower post-pit (half-sectioned to show position of the post). Friernhay Street. 20cm scale. (© RAMM)

Figure 34. Top: Roadworks trench which exposed the north-western corner of the fortress defences at the corner of Upper Paul Street and Gandy Street. On the left of the Museum side entrance is Neil Holbrook. Bottom: by coincidence, the course the outer lip of the ditch matches the run of kerb stones. 2m scale. (© RAMM)

clearly be seen following excavation, represented by different coloured square blocks at the Roman ground level. The stacks survived up to 11 courses high and were found to have been placed vertically rather than at an angle. This suggests that, at least in this section of the rampart, it may have been provided with a timber revetment on its front face, rather than the sloping turf front often shown in reconstruction drawings.

Remarkable at the above site was Henderson's prediction, before excavation began, that the below ground remains of an interval tower with the same dimensions as that seen at Friernhay Street, would be located at a spot that he pointed out to supervisor Mark Knight. The front two posts of the tower were duly found within 30cm of the forecast location. Modern granite posts still mark their position at the time of writing and the tower is shown as confirmed on Figure 27. Given that the spacing between the two interval towers found at Friernhay Street on the south-western defences was reckoned to be 99 Roman feet, how had Henderson managed to arrive with such unerring accuracy at his interval tower prediction on the opposite north-eastern defences? An astonishing 21 towers and corner towers spaced out along three separate different-facing lengths of the defences, stood on undulating ground between the two sites. In order for the calculation to work, each of these towers had to be positioned on plan as they would have been when the supporting posts were sunk at the original Roman ground surface level. A clear understanding of the terrain as it would have presented to the mid-first century Roman surveyors would have been necessary to achieve this.

The street system (more of the fortress plan revealed)

With all four sides of the fortress defences positioned by 1986 and the opposing south-western and north-eastern corners located by excavation, it became achievable for Henderson to estimate the size of the fortress and to begin to identify the positions of its four main gates. Key to this came with the recognition that a previously known Roman road, running from Topsham to the south-east gate of the Roman city, was perfectly aligned with one of the fortress streets. Henderson proposed that the continuous direct alignment of the Roman road and the known fortress street, demonstrated that the road from Topsham to Exeter was almost certainly planned and constructed contemporaneously with the establishment of the fortress. Not only this, but the road would have required a gateway at the point where it entered the fortress. By comparison with the standard fortress plan, it was clear that the road from Topsham entered the Exeter fortress at the *porta principalis sinistra;* likely to be the only gate on the south-east defences. This enabled Henderson to argue that the standard Roman fort plan could be applied and the crucial location of the T-junction between the two main streets of the *via principalis*

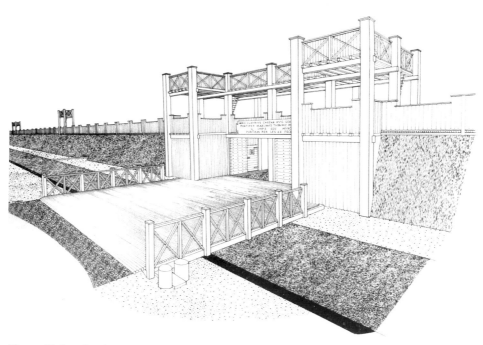

Figure 35. Imaginative reconstruction of the east gateway of the Neronian fortress at Usk, Wales. Drawing by Martin Dugdale (© W.H. Manning, University of Wales Press)

and the *via praetoria* could be pinpointed (see Figure 26). The approximate location of this spot in modern day Exeter is in the middle of Fore Street looking downhill towards the River Exe (standing there today however is not to be recommended – the bus to St Thomas and Alphington passes over it on a frequent basis). Fore Street thus preserves the line of the *via praetoria* leading from the headquarters building (*principia*) to the main gate of the fortress (the *porta praetoria*) facing towards the River Exe. The foundations of this gate in the form of massive post-holes may still survive today beneath Fore Street close to its junction with Friernhay Street (Figure 27). It may have looked something like the gateway shown in the reconstruction drawing of the east gateway at the Neronian fortress at Usk in Wales (Figure 35).

Cohort barracks (legionary accommodation)

By the time of the arrival of the legions in Britain the chief sub-unit of the legion was the cohort which comprised six centuries. We have seen previously that timber buildings first identified at the Goldsmith Street site had been identified as Roman legionary cohort barracks by 1973. It had become apparent that these barracks were grouped together in blocks of three facing pairs, each back-to-back pair separated from its neighbouring pair by a minor street. The arrangement of six paired barracks formed one cohort block. The legionary fortress of the mid-first century would conventionally have ten such cohort blocks occupying positions around the inner perimeter of the fortress defences; see Figure 26 for this arrangement where the blocks are known as *centuriae*. Figure 27 gives the known or suspected location of each of the ten cohort blocks at Exeter designated by the letters A-J, beginning with A in the top north-western corner of the fortress. Each individual barrack of a cohort block is numbered 1-6. Cohort block E would by custom have been allocated to the first cohort (the most prestigious of the ten); it occupied a prime position in the middle section of the fortress close to the headquarters building. The remains of post-trenches identified as those belonging to timber barracks have been found associated with all of the cohort blocks at the Exeter fortress with the exception of Blocks E and F.

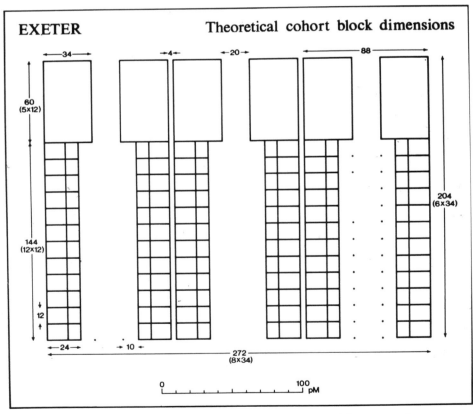

Figure 36. Theoretical plan of an Exeter legionary cohort block by C.G. Henderson. Scale in Roman feet (*pes Monetalis*). (© RAMM)

Recognising all of this, Henderson applied the same exercise in metrical analysis that he had undertaken for the 'blueprint' plan of the fortress, albeit at a different scale. Once again, using the Roman foot (*pes Monetalis*) for the basis of his calculations, he produced a theoretical plan of a standard cohort block of six barracks as it might have appeared on the ground at the Exeter fortress (Figure 36). Each barrack could hold a century of 80 men. The term century had been retained from the citizen army of the Republican era even though it had for some time been applied to the 80-man century of the professional Roman army. This permanent army had come into being around the turn of the first century BC and thus long before the arrival of the legions in Britain. The 80-man century was further divided into ten squads of eight men. Each squad was known as a *contubernium* (see above and Figure 22). This name was applied also to the room in which each eight-man group occupied within a barrack. Where excavation of individual cohort barracks has taken place, the outer walls and the central spine wall of the barrack can be identified by their parallel post-trenches as seen in Barracks 2 and 3 of Cohort Block C at Goldsmith Street

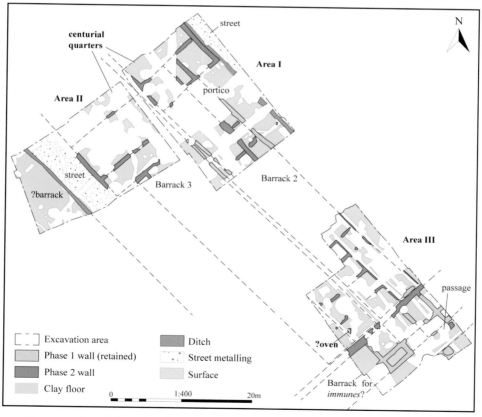

Figure 37. Plan of the cohort barracks 2 and 3 (and the *immunes* barrack to their rear) at Goldsmith Street 1971. Drawn by David Gould. (© Cotswold Archaeology)

(Figure 37). The Goldsmith Street barracks were rebuilt during their lifetime but their basic layout and overall dimensions remained consistent. The shallower and more ephemeral room partitions are sometimes apparent as was the case at the Bartholomew Street East site (see Figure 38).

Figure 39 shows a cut-away drawing of the *contubernia* within a barrack block. The soldiers shown in the figure are auxiliaries in a fort barrack rather than legionaries, but the arrangement of the rooms is the same for legionary and auxiliary infantry. Each room was sub-divided into two with an inner accommodation area and an outer smaller space for the storage of weapons and shields. The shields of the legionaries at Exeter were probably of the type seen in Figure 40; when stored they could have been nested together to save space. Bunk beds would have been in place within the area allocated to the sleeping quarters with a 'hot-bed' system probably in operation.

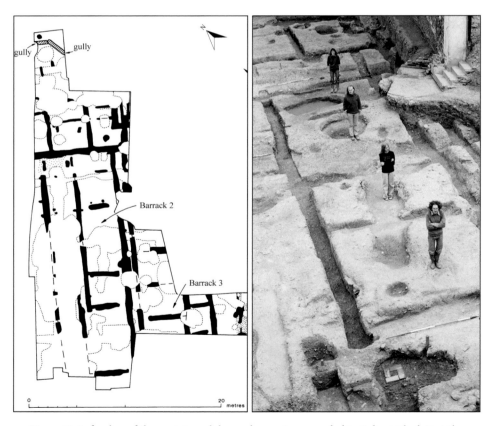

Figure 38. Left: plan of the post-trench barrack remains recorded in Cohort Block G at the Bartholomew Street East site. Right: an excavator stands in each of the rear four *contubernia* of Barrack Block 2. (© RAMM)

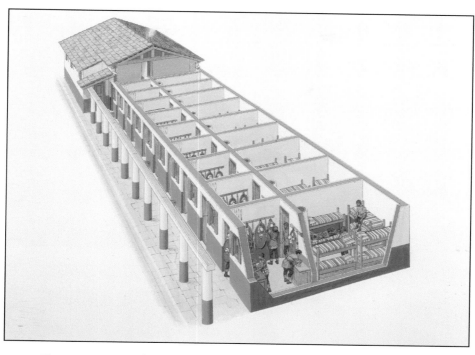

Figure 39. Cut away drawing of a barrack to reveal the rooms of the *contubernia*.
(© akg-images /Peter Connolly)

Each century was led by a centurion who would choose an *optio* to be his second in command should he fall ill or become incapacitated. The spacious centurial quarters occupied the large room at the head of each barrack, whilst the *optio* may sometimes have taken the tail-end room of the barrack to 'bookend' the centurion at the head. The presence of a clay floor, and at one stage an oven, in the end *contubernium* of Barrack 3 within Cohort Block C (Figure 37) suggests that this room might have had some special status and the presence of the *optio* in this room may have been the reason.

Figure 40. Replica shield (*scutum*) of the type used by legionaries. Note that the shield has seen 'action' with the boss of the shield having been used in attack. (Photo John Pamment Salvatore)

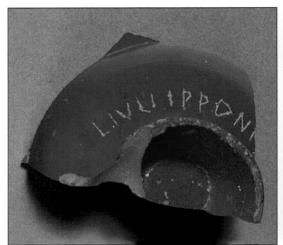

Figure 41. Left: a Samian cup base with the graffito of *L IVLI IPPONIA*: Restored as the property of LUCIUS JULIUS HIPPONICUS. (© RAMM) Right: modern day cup - property of Sarah!

Figure 42. Re-enactment group from *Legio Secunda Augusta* (UK) and *Legio Secunda Augusta* (Netherlands).They are portraying legionary soldiers of the mid-to-late 1st century AD. (author's collection)

We know the name of one of the legionaries from Cohort Block C. *Lucius Julius Hipponicus* scratched his name on the base of a Samian cup (Figure 41) no doubt to prevent it from going astray (an office worker today might purchase a 'named' mug for the same reason). *Hipponicus* would have looked like one of the legionaries depicted as part of a century ordered up behind its centurion and a standard bearer (*signifier*) of *Legio II Augusta* (*LEG II AVG*) in Figure 42.

The metalworking shop (*fabrica*) and workers accommodation

The *fabrica* (metal-working shop), probably took the form of a large square courtyard building with ranges of rooms on all four sides. It occupied a plot between the barracks of Cohorts E and C (see Figure 27). During excavation in 1973, it was quickly apparent that we were not dealing with the post-trenches of a barrack block but those of a much more substantial building. In addition to the deep and wide outer wall trenches (Figure 43) there were twinned pairs of internal post-pits intended to hold the massive posts (thicker in girth than modern telegraph poles) necessary to support the roof of a building of at least two storeys in height (Figure 44).

Comparison of the plan of this building with one of similar function recorded at the Inchtuthil legionary fortress in Scotland showed it to be an aisled hall. The building almost certainly incorporated a clerestory (a window running

Figure 43. Deep post-trench of the outer wall of the aisled hall (*fabrica*) at Trichay Street 1972. 30cm scale. (© RAMM)

Figure 44. The excavated interior of the aisled hall of the *fabrica* with its twined internal post-pits marked with red spots. Looking south-east. 2m scale. (© RAMM)

Figure 45. Conjectural reconstruction drawing of the aisled hall (*fabrica*) at Exeter. Drawn by
Roger Oram for Paul Bidwell. (© RAMM). Note the twinned post-pits for roof supports

around a high wall just below the roof line). The site evidence allowed Paul
Bidwell to offer a conjectural reconstruction of the building (Figure 45). The
interpretation of the aisled hall as a metal-working shop was confirmed by the
finding on the floor of the building of much metallic debris – including slag
and bronze-working offcuts. Lathes mounted on workbenches can be implied
by the shallow, plank-lined troughs set into the floor and intended to catch
the bronze metal waste beneath the lathes for recycling. The clerestory, if it
were simply a gap at eaves level rather than being glazed, would have provided
additional lighting and probably allowed the venting of rising hot air from
the smithing process. The room at the front, which faced onto a minor street,
produced no similar evidence of manufacture but was suggested instead to be
a storeroom. A shallow trench running around the inside of the room may have
supported cupboards or shelves where finished goods could be stored. Analysis

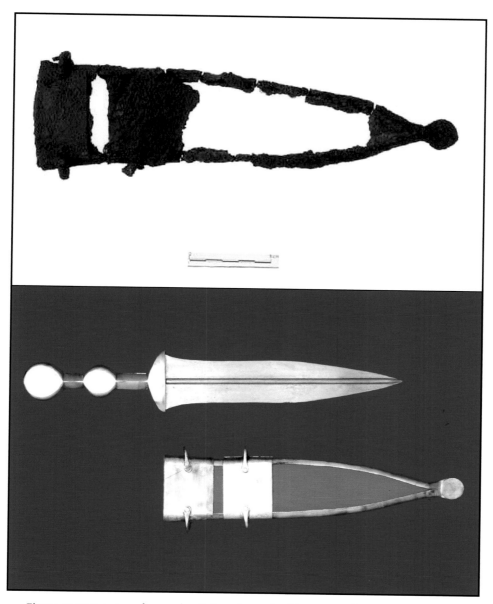

Figure 46. Top: an iron dagger sheath found near the *fabrica* at Trichay Street, 5cm scale. Bottom: a reproduction sheath and dagger (*pugio*) on display at the RAMM, Exeter. (© RAMM)

of the metal residues recovered in excavation showed that the bays within the aisled hall had been used for the manufacture of both iron and copper alloy objects. An iron sheath for a dagger (*pugio*) was found discarded in a dump of material near the *fabrica*. This was used in the reconstruction for museum purposes of both the dagger and its sheath (Figure 46).

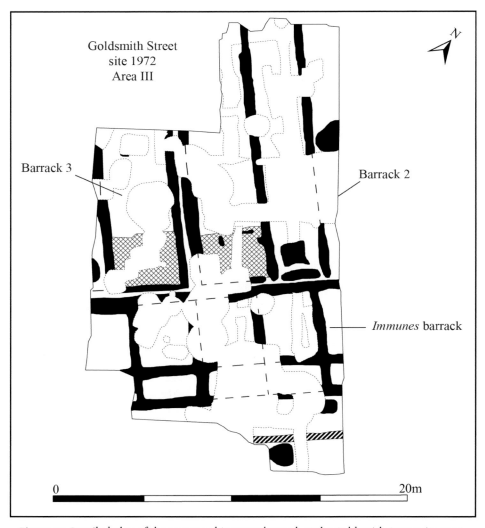

Figure 47. Detailed plan of the suspected *immunes* barrack at the Goldsmith Street site 1972.
(© RAMM). Redrawn by David Gould

Discovered in close proximity to the *fabrica* behind Cohort Block C at Goldsmith Street was a barrack which did not belong within a conventional cohort block (Figure 47). This barrack was believed to have provided accommodation for non-combatant soldiers known as *immunes.* It was separated from a similar parallel barrack only by a narrow passage. No assembly and mustering of troops for roll call would have been possible in this restricted space. This stands in contrast to the arrangement at a cohort block where a street separated each back-to-back pair of barracks. In addition, the space allotted for the front section of each *contubernium* of the *immunes* barrack was considerably smaller than that within a legionary barrack. Probably because bulky shields and weapons were not stored there but the tools of individual craftsmen of various proficiencies engaged solely on specialised tasks. Those engaged in metalworking were known as *fabri* and they may have occupied the non-cohort barracks adjacent to their workplace in the nearby *fabrica* (see Figure 27 above).

The legionary bathhouse

The legionary bathhouse at Exeter was excavated, as we have seen in Chapter 1, primarily in the years 1971-72. Figure 48 shows the extent of the excavation in front of the Cathedral. The bathhouse was the only building known to have been completed in stone within the otherwise wooden establishment. It was also constructed within a pre-selected plot that was likely to have been occupied by a smaller timber bathhouse during the first years of the occupation of the fortress. The plot occupied a total area of some 4,000m². According to the excavator Paul Bidwell, the bathhouse was constructed in the years AD 60-65, and along with the Temple of Claudius at Colchester it would have been one of the first monumental masonry buildings to have been erected in Britain, and certainly the first in the South-West. The three major rooms of the bathhouse building were the *frigidarium* (cold room), the *tepidarium* (warm room) and the *caldarium* (hot room). The Roman bathing practice of the times was thought to involve the bather progressing through the various rooms into the *caldarium* where the heat would open up the pores of the skin. Dirt and sweat were scraped away with metal implements called *strigils*. The bather could subsequently rub oils into the cleansed skin before exiting back through the tepidarium into the unheated *frigidarium* where the skin's pores would close-up trapping the oils. Hot and cold plunge baths and basins were also provided. Outer clothing was retrieved from a covered changing room called an *apodyterium*. Beyond the walls of the bathhouse an external exercise yard (*palaestra*) provided space for games and sports such as wrestling.

The entire hot room and part of the warm room were revealed in excavation (Figure 49). Bidwell described the bathhouse in detail in his 1979 volume on the subject. He found that the hypocaust (a system in which hot air circulated beneath a raised floor known as a *suspensura*) had once existed in both the hot room and warm room. The hypocaust floor had been destroyed when the building was later converted (see below Chapter 7). The fired-clay tile stacks (known as *pilae*) upon which the floor was supported had survived the demolition for the most part; these may be seen in ordered rows on Figure 50. The relatively lower temperature of the warm room was achieved by placing small arches beneath the wall separating the hot room from the warm room; these acted to control the amount of heated air reaching the warm room (Figure 51). Much of the furnace which heated the hot room on its south-western side was exposed in excavation (Figure 52). A twin furnace is assumed to have existed on the opposite side of the hot room. The

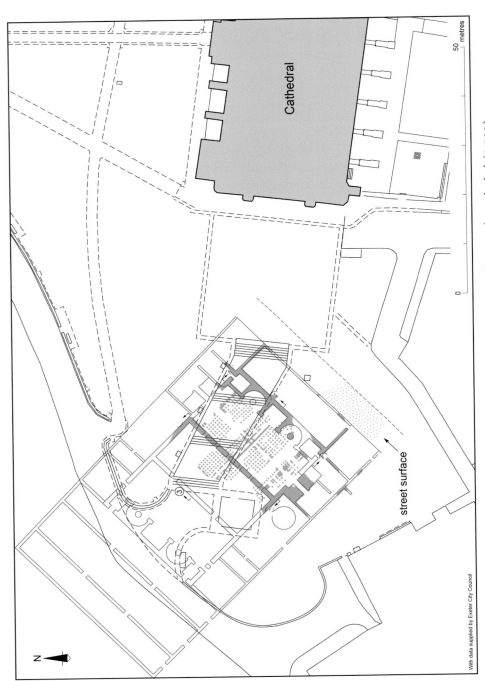

Figure 48. Plan of the excavated remains of the bathhouse in relation to the Cathedral. (© ECC.)

Figure 49. The *caldarium* (hot room) of the legionary bathhouse looking south-east. The tile stacks of the below-floor hypocaust system are revealed, The massive walls of the later basilica overlay them. 2m scale. (© RAMM)

Figure 50. Rows of tile stacks (*pilae*) which supported the floor (*suspensura*) of the *caldarium*. 30cm scale. (© RAMM)

Figure 51. One of the arches which allowed a restricted flow of hot air from the hot room (*caldarium*) to circulate through to the warm room (*tepidarium*). (© RAMM)

Figure 52. Detail of the south-west furnace flue which fed hot air to circulate beneath the floor of the *caldarium*. It also heated a hot water boiler mounted above it. 2m scale. (© RAMM)

furnaces provided the hot air which was driven by natural processes to circulate beneath the suspended floor before it rose up through hollow box tiles within the walls to vent just below the roof line. The water supply to the fortress and its bathhouse would have been brought in from the nearest sources (modern day St Sidwell) by means of a wooden aqueduct to connect with a piped system. However, precisely where it entered the fortress is not known. Possibly, it could have been engineered to cross the defences at the rear gate of the fortress and run down to discharge into the various boilers and pools of the bathhouse. Figure 53 shows a conjectural drawing of the hot-water boiler which would have been located above the furnace. It has been estimated that the bathhouse would have required 70,000 gallons of water each day. The waste run-off was channelled down to the River Exe by way of a man-made watercourse which ran parallel to the Coombe stream; this is where Lower Coombe Street is today.

Bidwell believed that the Exeter baths, particularly with their emphasis on symmetry, was an advanced design which pre-empted later grand 'Imperial-type' bathhouses found in Rome itself. In his view, highly experienced architects would have been brought in to oversee the complex building project which, due to its size, would have required advanced constructional techniques. These same architects may have been involved in the design and build of a very similar bathhouse at Caerleon in Wales where *Legio II Augusta* are known to have been stationed after they left Exeter around AD 75 – see below. The excavator at Caerleon, David Zienkiewicz, undertook a metrological analysis of the bathhouse design at Caerleon. Chris Henderson carried out

Figure 53. Conjectural reconstruction drawing of the south-west furnace house of the *caldarium*. Drawn by Eric W. Haddon. (© RAMM)

a similar exercise and produced a reconstructed plan and elevation of the Exeter bathhouse (Figure 54). Figure 55 is a cut-away model of the hot room (*caldarium*) which provides some idea of the opulence and grandeur of the building, although in reality the interior would most likely have been obscured by a haze of steam.

The bathhouse was constructed of local purple-coloured trap (volcanic stone) from the Rougemont Hill quarry which, at the time of the building's construction was outside of the legionary defences but which was later incorporated within the town wall circuit. No expense was spared on furnishings; Purbeck Marble

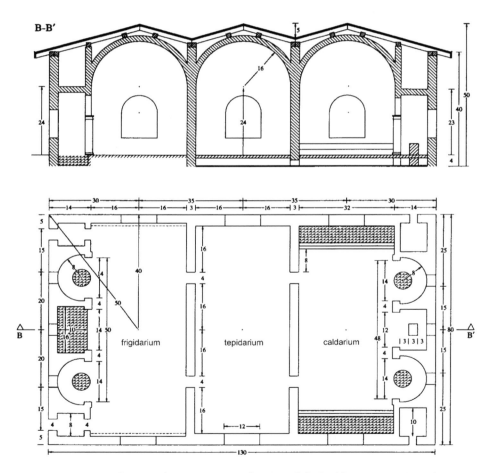

Figure 54. Architectural reconstruction drawing of the bathhouse as envisaged by C.G. Henderson. Dimensions are in Roman feet (*pes Monetalis*). Drawn by T. Ives (© RAMM)

Figure 55. A cut-away model of the bathhouse *caldarium* by Eric W. Haddon. (© RAMM)

was employed for basins (*labra*) and mouldings (Figure 56) whilst some of the floors appear to have been paved with polychrome mosaic – believed to be the earliest known examples from Britain (Figure 57). Black and white stone tiles provided the finish for the hypocaust floor and the interior walls were adorned with painted wall-plaster. Hollow box tiles placed in the bathhouse walls, allowed hot air to heat the walls and rise up to vent at roof level (Figure 58). Both flat and domed glass widows allowed natural daylight to enter (the windows were likely to be the first to appear in Britain). Lead for pipe-work was probably sourced from the Mendip Hills; iron came from the Blackdown Hills to the east of Exeter. The roof would have been tiled in the Roman manner (see Figure 59) with the overhang finished with decorated moulded tile plaques (*antefixa*). One antefix from the Exeter bathhouse portrays a human face framed by hair, the design possibly deriving from classical images of a gorgon (Figure 60). They acted to protect the building in a similar fashion to the gargoyles seen on medieval churches and cathedrals. Another theme portrayed was a pair of dolphins either side of a rosette (see tilery discussion below).

Labra: Exeter, Pompeii and Herculaneum

Figure 56. Purbeck standing marble basin (*labrum*) rim from the Exeter bathhouse (top left) plus complete examples from Pompeii and Herculaneum. (© RAMM and John Allan)

Figure 57. Fragment of polychrome mosaic from the legionary bathhouse. (© RAMM)

Figure 58. Box tile, employed in heating the walls of the bathhouse. 5cm scale. (© RAMM)

Figure 59. Roman roofing tiles shown in the arrangement in which they would have been fitted on the bathhouse roof (Wikimedia Commons, photo: Immanuel Giel)

Figure 60. An antefix of the type found at the bathhouse. It depicts what appears to be a female face derived from classical *gorgoneia*. This example from the St Loye's site is blackened by wood smoke from its likely proximity to a furnace vent or chimney at roof level. 10cm scale. (© RAMM)

The headquarters building (*principia*)

The middle section of the fortress was reserved for high status buildings. Principal amongst these was the headquarters building known as the *principia*. Its position, in a central and dominant position within the fortress at the head of the main street running from the front gate, can be identified by reference to Figure 27. Virtually nothing of the building has ever been seen in excavation, other than a run of large posts, evident by their postholes. They had been driven into the ground, probably with the employment of a pile-driver. Pile-drivers and cranes were known to have been used by the Roman army for building projects including bridges. Apart from the bathhouse, the *principia* would have been one of the largest buildings in the fortress. It probably took the form of a massive building of timber-frame construction arranged with rooms around three sides of a courtyard. Rendered with plaster it would have been two storeys in height. Figure 61 conjures up a picture of the construction of the headquarters building towering above a barrack block being erected in the foreground. The *principia* was the administrative and religious focus of the fortress. The rear range of

Figure 61. Imaginative illustration of the construction of a legionary timber barrack (foreground) and the headquarters building (*principia*) behind. The panels of the *principia* are being rendered with plaster (© akg-images/Peter Connolly)

rooms would have held at their centre the regimental shrine known as the *aedes* which housed the standard bearing the legionary eagle. The pay chest was often kept close to this sacred place. The legionary commander (legate) would have an office in the *principia* as would his second in command (*tribunus laticlavius*) and the camp prefect (*praefectus castrorum*), who oversaw the maintenance of the camp and its defences and supervised engineering and construction projects. Other offices would have been required, including a *tabularium,* a room where a senior clerk would keep account of individual service and pay records, guard duties and day-to-day rosters.

Other specialised buildings

Immediately adjacent to the *principia* would have stood the *praetorium* which was the personal house of the legionary commander and his family. Only senior officers of the legion were allowed wives and family within the confines of the fortress (at this date legionaries were barred from entering into an official marriage contract). Befitting his status, the legate would have been provided with a large well-appointed courtyard house likely to have been of Mediterranean appearance despite the British climate. At Exeter, Bidwell has argued that the *praetorium* stood to one side of the *principia* (see Figure 27) separated from it by a street. This was on the basis of excavation undertaken by Lady Fox in South St in 1945 which produced evidence of a house constructed with the same driven-post technique as that used for the *principia.* If it was the *praetorium* then Lady Fox may have exposed part of one range. The presence of ceramic roofing tile in the recovered occupation layers do suggest a high-quality building of some significance; the barracks and lesser buildings on the other hand were probably roofed with wooden shingles which have not survived.

In a conventional fortress plan, and Exeter appears largely to obey the rules, the houses of the senior officers (tribunes) would have been facing onto the *via principalis* and opposite Cohort Blocks E and F (see Figure 27). They are likely to have been courtyard houses similar in Mediterranean architectural style to that of the commander's house but of lesser grandeur. Part of one of a suspected tribune's house was seen in section only opposite Cohort Block E at Mary Arches Street in 1975.

We shall see in a later chapter that foodstuffs and other supplies arrived at the fortress by road from sites which lay beyond the defences. However, a sufficient quantity of grain stored within the fortress appears to be a pre-requisite at Exeter and other fortresses of the same period. Granaries leave a unique archaeological marker in the ground as the floor of the building will be raised up on closely spaced wooden piles within a grid. Air circulating beneath the raised floor assists in keeping the commodity (probably wheat and/or barley) from becoming spoiled by damp or easily reached by rodents. Just such an array of pile-driven posts forming a regularly spaced grid was revealed in an excavation in 1973, at 196-97 High Street, prior to the demolition of these buildings as part of the Guildhall Shopping Centre development.

The Tilery

The main source of clay, and the place of manufacture of tiles for the fortress baths, appears to have been a tilery located outside of the north-east defences where modern Princesshay now stands. A huge number of tiles would have been required in the bathhouse construction for the roof and hypocaust system (see above). It was evidently common practice for the terracotta tiles to be left out in the open sun before final firing; animal paw prints are often encountered on the finished articles. An exceptional find from the bathhouse was one tile which had been used for a writing exercise. Letters of the Latin alphabet were inscribed on the tile whilst the clay was still wet (Figure 62).

When the legion left Exeter for Caerleon around AD 75 (see below), the legionary tile maker must have taken with him to Caerleon the moulds used to produce the various decorative tile antefixes which adorned the roof of the Exeter bathhouse. One of these moulds was found to have been employed in the production of a 'dolphin' antefix, identical examples of which have been found both at Exeter and Caerleon (Figure 63). Caerleon is attested epigraphically as a base of the Second Augustan Legion where the legion is mentioned on many gravestones including that of a 100-year-old veteran legionary of *II Augusta* (Figure 64). The antefix mould link provides proof positive that the legion was

Figure 62. A *pila* tile with an alphabet graffito inscribed before final firing. 10cm scale. (© RAMM)

Figure 63. Dolphin *antefixa* from the same mould recovered at both Exeter and Caerleon.
Left: fragments from the Exeter bathhouse. Right: replica from Caerleon (© RAMM)

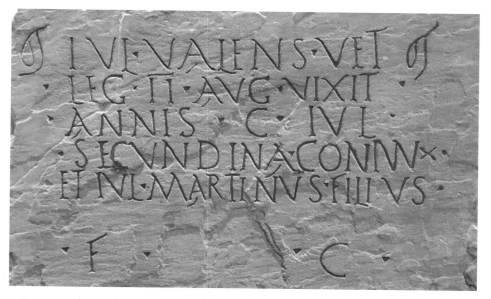

Figure 64. The Caerleon gravestone of 100-year-old veteran Julius Valens of *Legio II Augusta*.
His wife Secundina and his and son Martinus set it up (author's collection)

indeed the garrison force at Exeter, despite no inscriptions bearing the title of *Legio II Augusta* (or its commonly abbreviated form *LEG II AVG*) ever having been found here.

Summary

The evidence from excavation suggests that the fortress must have been a busy and noisy place with the various workshops operating throughout the day and carts arriving and departing from the granary. Roll calls, inspections, and troop assemblages for engineering and building projects either within or outside of the fortress, would have been a regular occurrence. The construction of the bathhouse would of course have been a major event and labour intensive, involving the dressing of countless blocks of masonry quarried from Rougemont where Exeter's later Norman castle was built. As a military establishment security and discipline are likely to have rigorously enforced. Entry into the fortress would have been strictly controlled whilst the legionaries will have been furnished with the password of the day. Falling asleep on duty is likely to have been punishable by death. Those committing less serious misdemeanours would receive a blow from the centurion's heavy vine stick which he carried as a staff of office. The only civilians living permanently within the confines of the fortress would have been the wives and children of the senior officers and any of their household slaves.

Chapter 4

The purpose of the legionary fortress and its period of occupation

'May the soldier bear arms only to check the armed aggressor and may the fierce trumpet blare for naught but solemn pomp! ......and if there be any land that feared not Rome, may it love Rome instead'.

Ovid, Fasti, Book I (early first century AD)

Real and perceived power

In common with nearly all new territory acquired by Rome, the South-West would have been expected to become 'Romanised'. This would see the adoption of a monetised Roman market economy, bringing with it governance and taxation based upon the Roman model. Central to this policy was the integration of local elites to assist in the governing of the region, whose boundaries were often, but not exclusively, based on those of the pre-Roman population. The acquisition of enhanced social status and material benefits, bestowed by the Roman State upon those who had influence in freshly occupied lands, was known to be effective in countering any thoughts of mounting a resistance. Quite how successfully this integration of a local elite was achieved initially in the far South-West is unclear. As we have seen above, the territory of the Dumnonii is difficult to determine. The areas to the east of the Blackdown Hills in Devon and the Quantock Hills in Somerset would seem to fall within the Durotrigian tribal domain where locally minted coinage was in use before the Roman invasion. An economy based on coinage would demand a community with a joint purpose and presumably a powerful elite capable of producing the coinage and controlling the area in which it circulated. The entire South-West

Peninsula to the west of the Quantocks and the Blackdown Hills on the other hand, seemingly had no such economic tradition based on a regionally minted coinage. Without this to bind them in a shared purpose then more localised groups may have dominated. This may have resulted in little sense of a wider tribal identity in the South-West at the time of the Roman arrival.

Nevertheless, if anyone of influence amongst the local population of what the Romans State defined as Dumnonia was indeed called upon to negotiate the future relationship between their peoples and the Roman administration to which they would henceforth be subject, then the fortress would have provided an impressive meeting venue. Edward Luttwak has commented that:*'...the dominant dimension of power was not physical but psychological, the product of others perception of Roman strength rather than the use of this strength'*. As a physical manifestation of Rome's power, a visitor, upon entering the main gate (having approached from the River Exe) could not fail but to have been impressed by the legionary headquarters building at the top of the hill (this is where modern Fore Street meets the junction with North Street and South Street).. Totally alien in its architecture, and probably rendered to give an appearance of stone, it would be like nothing seen before in the South-West. Furthermore, the stone-built bathhouse would be an imposing and recognisably grandiose building if one were to view it in its present location today, let alone 2,000 years ago. De Laine in 1999, stated that the architectural elaboration found in the Exeter baths belongs with a group of buildings which are show-pieces of Roman power in newly acquired territory. In this respect, the fortress at Exeter, as a demonstration of Roman capabilities, might be regarded as having had an underlying role in the process of the subjugation of the region. Figure 65 attempts to show something of the scale of the bathhouse in comparison to modern buildings nearby. Only the Cathedral will be appreciably larger.

Period of occupation

When the fortress was constructed around AD 55 it may have been intended as a permanent legionary base in the South-West for the Second Augustan Legion. The building of a stone bathhouse on a pre-selected plot within the fortress would appear to confirm this. It will be apparent that the bathhouse played an important role in the day-to-day operations of the fortress. The baths were large enough to be used by several hundred bathers at one time – the numbers commensurate with the needs of the 5,000-plus legionary garrison. It would have provided a place to relax and socialise; the equivalent of a modern-day combined spa and leisure centre. The high standard of provision and considerations of well-being for the soldiers of the permanent garrison would have engendered a sense of loyalty to the legion and the Emperor. This,

Figure 65. An architectural 'skeleton' view of the bathhouse against a 1970s backdrop gives some idea of scale. Only the Cathedral is an appreciably larger building. (© RAMM)

in some measure would compensate for the loss of family life. Legionaries were forbidden by law to contract a marriage whilst serving (this restriction lasted until AD 197 and the reign of Septimius Severus). Common-law wives and any resulting children were tolerated however if they lived outside of the fortress. A handsome gratuity of land or money (or sometimes both) awaited those who completed their term of service (thought to be 25 years at enlistment). The wives and children of these retiring legionaries would automatically become Roman citizens and it was not uncommon for male offspring of a suitable age to be recruited into the army at this point.

Whilst residing at the Exeter fortress the garrison would have been involved not only in the construction of its own bathhouse, but also in the provision of bridges and roads across the region as part of the vital process of Romanisation. Computer generated terrain modelling work by Exeter University published in 2023 predicted a wide network of Roman roads across the South-West. Some of these have been located by LiDAR (Light Detection And Radar) and are seen also as cropmarks on satellite imagery (Figure 66). Whilst not all roads will be military in origin, it may be suspected that many are.

In the event, the legion (or rather the greater part of it) was transferred away from its Exeter base around AD 75. The reason for this redeployment was one primarily dictated by pressing military requirements elsewhere. The Emperor Vespasian instructed the governor of Britain from AD 74-78, Julius Frontinus,

Figure 66. A Roman road with parallel side ditches at Middledown, Bow, Devon, revealed as a cropmark on a satellite photo (image reproduced from Google Earth Pro 2011 by S. Kaye)

to undertake major campaigns in the north of Britain and to complete the subjugation of Wales. Vespasian's old legion, the Second Augusta, were chosen to assist in the Welsh campaign. At that date, the area west of Exeter may still not have been totally secure, as the continued presence of auxiliary forts in central Devon and Cornwall after the legionary withdrawal attests. For example, the *vicus* (civilian settlement) outside the fort at Okehampton (and by extension the fort itself) can be shown by pottery evidence to have been occupied into the early years of the 80s AD.

Arriving in Caerleon in South Wales, within the territory of the troublesome Silures, the Second Augusta constructed a fortress (*Isca Silurum*) on the west bank of the River Usk. The legion went on to retain their Caerleon base well into the late Roman period. During their long tenure the initial wooden fortress and its earth rampart defences were converted to stone, the remains of which, such as the barracks with their individual *contubernia*, can be seen today (Figure 67). Had the legion stayed at Exeter and not been subject to redeployment then the fortress would surely have undergone the same development as that which took place at Caerleon, and the timber barracks would have been replaced in stone to join the bathhouse in that distinction.

Figure 67. A stone-built barrack of *Legio II Augusta* at the Caerleon legionary fortress in Wales.
(© Nigel Mykura and licenced for reuse under cc-by-sa/2.0)

Chapter 5

Extra-mural sites of the *prata legionum*

'That a base should be established at Topsham at an early date need therefore, cause no surprise'.

C.A.Ralegh Radford 1937

It is impossible to talk of the legionary fortress at Exeter in isolation. It was at the hub of an integrated system of establishments of different sizes and purpose, some purely military, some civilian, but all acting in concert to advance the prosperity of the region and the wider aims of the Empire. The fortress would have provided the focal point for a coherent system of auxiliary forts placed at strategic locations controlling routes in and out of the South-Western Peninsula. Rome relied on auxiliary forces drawn from across the Empire to police its territory and to assist in campaigns. They were organised in cohorts of smaller numbers than a legion, commonly around 500 or 1,000 strong, in units of different composition. For example, some were all infantry and some were all cavalry units, together with hybrid units which were part mounted and part infantry. The deployment of any one type of auxiliary unit might depend upon the local topography or the level of potential hostility to the Roman presence, or a combination of both. In addition to the policing role they also introduced highly visible signs of the Roman way of life with settlements emerging outside the forts and alongside the military roads; such settlements encouraged local trade. Excavation just beyond the defences at the fort at Okehampton demonstrated a thriving civilian community whilst the fort was in occupation. The forts were not necessarily all contemporary and some clearly had more than one phase, perhaps marking an intervening gap between occupation or a change of unit. All of them were connected by a network of roads leading back ultimately to the legionary base at Exeter. It is not possible, within the scope of this book, to discuss the role of the outlying forts in any detail. It is, however, necessary to look at those sites of the Roman military period which existed in very close proximity to Exeter and to attempt to understand their relationship with the fortress.

A legion commanded by the legate of the emperor could possess territory on behalf of the Roman people. The existence of these legionary territories (known as *prata legionis*, literally: the pastures or meadows of the legions) is well attested across the Empire. Their purpose, initially and primarily, was to provide grazing for the pack-animals and horses maintained by the legion once it had secured its chosen location as a base of operations. Where a timber fortress was to be erected, the appropriated land would have incorporated locally available raw materials necessary for its construction. Sufficient areas of woodland for the provision of timber would have been one obvious resource to which the army would have laid claim. David Mason, who made a study of *prata legionis* in Britain, stated: '*At Exeter, it seems logical to assume that the bulk of the prata legionum lay in the valley of the Exe, almost certainly extending as far as Topsham*'. Whether the legionary territory may have encompassed an area much wider than this is open to conjecture; each legion's requirements would have been different dependent upon the surrounding topography, the availability of resources and even perhaps local political factors. Henrietta Quinnell has suggested that any defined territory officially designated for the support of the legion at Exeter might have included the agriculturally rich land of the lower Exe Valley to the east and north of the fortress.

The types of establishment which emerged within the immediate hinterland of Exeter were diverse. Paul Bidwell called these extra-mural sites 'satellite sites'. He saw them as places either under direct military control or with civilian populations which could be granted limited or complete autonomy. A number of predominantly civilian sites are now known to have existed alongside the Roman military road which led from the south-east gate of the fortress to the head of the river Exe estuary to the north-west of modern-day Topsham (Figure 68). Settlement areas immediately outside the fortress defences are generally known as *canabae* (more correctly, *canabae legionis* - a term applied specifically to the houses and workplaces of civilian traders, artisans and camp followers operating in commercial support of the legion). The unofficial families of legionaries might also be found in the *canabae*.

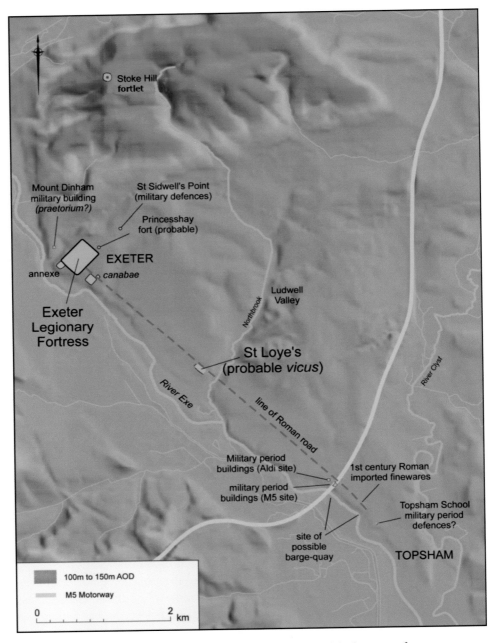

Figure 68. Roman military-period sites in the vicinity of the legionary fortress.
(© Stephen Kaye)

The *canabae (legionis)*

Over a period of two decades, beginning in the 1970s, several sites became available for excavation on the south-east side of the city as a result of road widening schemes or new housing developments at the top of Holloway Street/Topsham Road. The evidence from the various excavations suggests that we are looking at two detached sites beyond the south-east defences of the fortress. (Figure 69). The remains of timber buildings of a domestic and

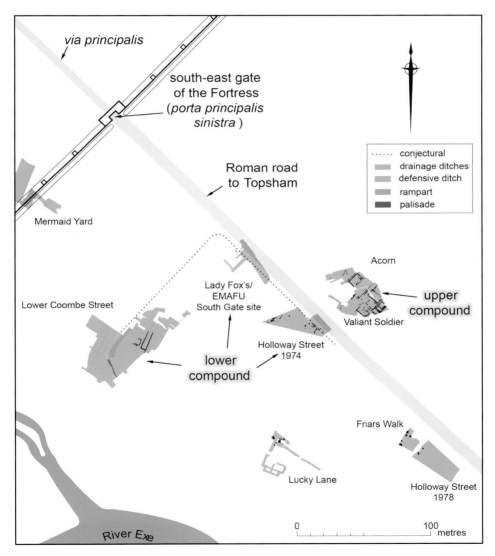

Figure 69. The location of the *canabae* sites immediately outside the south-east gate of the fortress. Drawn by Tony Ives (© ECC)

industrial nature were discovered on both sides of the Roman road. These buildings were identified by Paul Bidwell as being part of the *canabae*. The site at the higher elevation and to the north-east of the road is the upper compound, that to the south-west is the lower compound. Lady Fox's V-shaped 'fort' ditch seen in isolation in 1964 at her South Gate site now seems likely to be associated with the lower compound. The two compounds were found to be very different to each other in character and function, but both were occupied contemporaneously with the legionary occupation of the fortress (i.e. *c.* AD 55-75).

The upper compound

The extent of the upper compound is unknown; any boundary features lie beyond the limits of excavation. The remains of four post-trench timber buildings were found at The Valiant Soldier and Acorn Roundabout sites during the extension of Western Way at the top of Holloway Street (Figure 70). The four buildings were all well-constructed and may be described as domestic in nature, possessing in some cases small individual gravel courtyards. Buildings 1-3 were separated from Building 4 by a street or trackway defined by parallel wooden fences. The site had been carefully prepared. Evidence of turf and tree removal was recorded. A slight downward slope towards the south-west and the Roman road had been levelled by the deposition of clay and gravel before the building trenches were put in place. The post-trench technique (see above) was used in the building construction whilst specially prepared courtyard surfaces were sunk into the artificially levelled platform. This demonstrates a high degree of care and attention given to the construction programme. Buildings 1-3 were complex and displayed evidence of internal changes which had taken place over time. Small-scale extensions and partial re-building also took place during their lifetime. Significantly, Buildings 1-3 possessed fence-lines which hint at some segregation between the buildings themselves and may point to separate ownership. The lack of a regimented layout, coupled with the apparent propensity of the occupants to make changes over the course of the life of the buildings, lends weight to the idea that they may have been relatively well-appointed private living quarters. What is abundantly clear is that the irregular room plans stand in stark contrast to the uniformity of accommodation found in the barracks of the fortress.

The lower compound

The lower compound was found to have been enclosed by a variety of boundary features at different points on its circuit (Figure 69). Where the compound fronted onto the Roman road at Holloway Street, evidence was recovered of

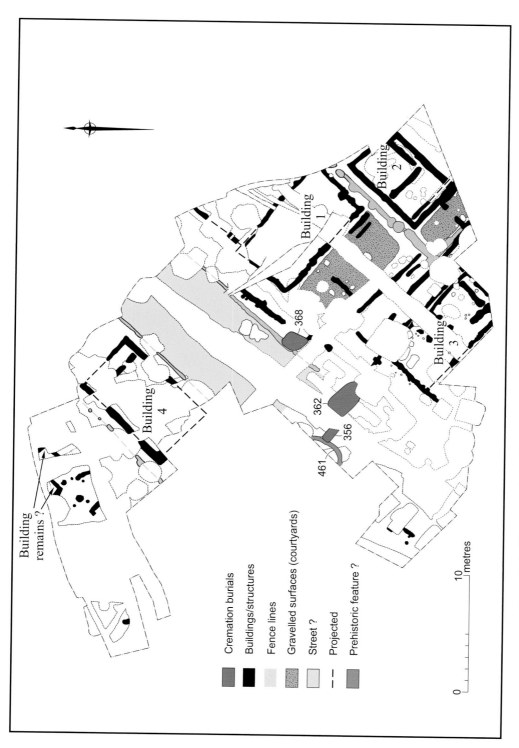

Figure 70. Buildings recorded in the upper compound of the *canabae*. Drawn by Tony Ives (© ECC)

a trench which once held a series of closely-spaced stakes. The archaeological feature may be interpreted as a wooden palisade fence which ran parallel with the road. A gateway in the fence provided access from the road into the compound. Successive phases of strip buildings located inside the fence on the Holloway Street sites may have been destroyed by accidental fire. Strip buildings were the standard form of accommodation for the civilian areas found outside forts and fortresses. Their uses were both commercial and domestic. An open-front allowed easy access to a shop or workshop at the front with living quarters at the back, often divided into small rooms. Copious amounts of charcoal, ash, burnt clay and iron slag in the building debris at the Holloway Street examples gives testimony to metal working, quite probably within the buildings themselves and a likely cause of the fires which destroyed them.

Part of the lower compound was identified in 1990 on the site of a multi-story car-park development further down the slope towards the River Exe at Lower Coombe Street. A stream flowed through the coombe in Roman times. The Roman army created a ditch from this stream and inserted a further parallel ditch to supplement the natural drainage flowing down to the River Exe. Figure 71/1-5 illustrates this and the development over time of this part of the lower compound, which was enclosed at its south-western corner by several successive man-made boundary features. The first clear indication of a defined enclosure boundary was a curving gully – too shallow to have any defensive function but highly reminiscent of the rounded corners of fort and fortress defences where these are seen in aerial photographs. Several phases of buildings (which have the appearance of workshops) were identified within. At various times, discrete areas were fenced off for what may have been any number of activities which have left almost no trace; the only clearly identifiable one being the mixing of mortar, possibly for roof-tile bedding. The shallow gulley was superseded by what might clearly be termed defensive features (Figure 71/6). A V-shaped ditch and rampart were introduced, along with a strong palisade fence (The ditch may be contemporary with the V-shaped ditch found by Lady Fox in 1964 at her South Gate site (Figure 69). These defensive features are discussed further in Chapter 6.

St Loye's civilian settlement (*vicus*)

Further along the Roman road from the *canabae,* and some 2.2 km from the fortress, a site which overlooked a crossing of the Northbrook stream was excavated by Marc Steinmetzer in 2010 at the former St Loye's College at Topsham Road (Figure 68 for location). The excavation did not extend to the road line, but Roman military-period buildings were found a short distance to its south-west with some in a more isolated location to the rear. The buildings

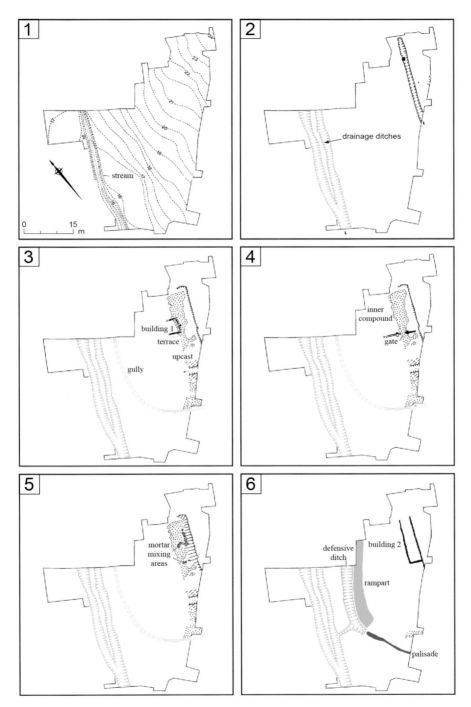

Figure 71. The development of the south-west corner of the lower compound at the Lower Coombe Street site. Drawn by Tony Ives. (© ECC). Re-drawn by David Gould

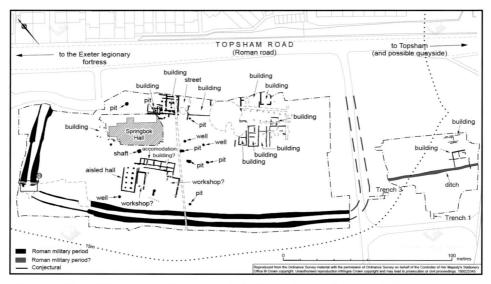

Figure 72. Plan of the Roman military-period civilian settlement (*vicus*) at the former St Loye's College on Topsham Road. Drawn by Tony Ives. (© ECC). Re-drawn by David Gould

were enclosed within parallel double-ditched defences which encompassed an area of about 1.6 ha (Figure 72). These defences were not necessarily in place at the outset of the establishment and their appearance at the site is discussed later. A few buildings outside of the defensive circuit on its south-eastern side were found by AC Archaeology in 2016 and appear also to be of the Roman military period. It is likely that the Roman site extended to the other side of the Topsham Road which is now occupied by a mid-20th century housing estate (Figure 73).

The recovered archaeology suggests a settlement (*vicus*) believed to be civilian in nature. (The term *vicus* has been employed as the settlement was not confined purely alongside the road, as would be the case with a linear settlement, but spread out behind the road. The buildings within the defences were dispersed with some areas apparently left empty. One group of buildings was found to have overlain a rectangular enclosure of the Late-pre-Roman Iron Age which had at its centre a roundhouse (Figure 74). It could be demonstrated archaeologically that the surrounding ditches of the late Iron Age enclosure were still open when they were deliberately infilled and sealed off in preparation for the Roman settlement that was to follow (Figure 75). The Roman operation to clear the site of native occupation is likely to have been achieved rapidly. Ditches left unattended and not maintained will very soon deteriorate and be subject to side slumping. Even one episode of rain can cause significant infill. The Iron Age enclosure ditches at St Loye's had, however,

Figure 73. A satellite image of the St Loye's site under excavation in 2010. The Burnthouse Lane Housing Estate is seen top right.(image: Bing Maps /Microsoft/Digital Globe)

acquired only a small amount of natural silt accumulation in their base before they were backfilled during what must have been a seizure of the land by the Roman army, followed by a landscaping exercise intended to prepare the site for the erection of timber buildings. Included within the backfill deposits of the Iron Age enclosure ditches were relatively large amounts of imported Samian ware, fine wares from Central Gaul, vessels with ritual connotations, and glass vessels (Figure 76). The event provides rare direct evidence of the impact of the mid-first century Roman occupation upon the indigenous Iron Age population; in this case occupying a site to the south-east of Exeter alongside the River Exe. Whether that intrusion was resisted is still a matter of conjecture; it is possible that the inhabitants were compensated and resettled elsewhere. What is certain, is that at least one Late Iron Age enclosure was given up by its occupants, either willingly or unwillingly, for the express purpose of the creation of a Roman settlement on the same site. This appears to have happened at a time when a sizeable Roman legionary presence would have been active in

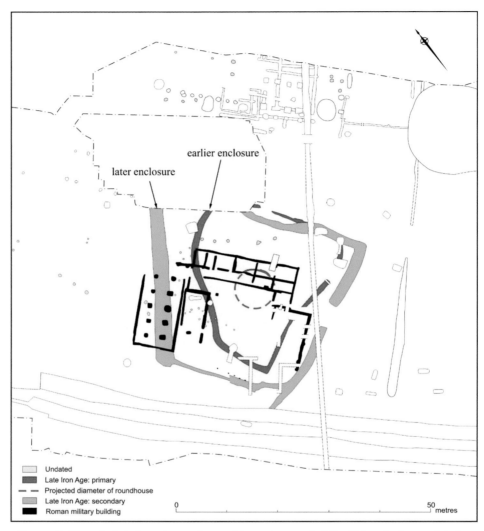

later enclosure

earlier enclosure

Undated
Late Iron Age: primary
Projected diameter of roundhouse
Late Iron Age: secondary
Roman military building

0   50
                                               metres

Figure 74. Plan of a Late Iron Age enclosure (shown in green) at the St Loye's site overlain by
Roman buildings. An earlier Iron Age enclosure is shown in red. (© ECC)

the area - with the fortress either completed or under construction at Exeter,
and legionary units working in the surrounding area, devoted to road building
and the creation of other infrastructure.

It is highly likely that the Roman army was responsible for the construction of
the buildings at the St Loye's settlement even if they were for civilian use. An
example of Roman military construction methods may be seen in the ground
plan of the complex of buildings which were erected on the site of the removed
and levelled Iron Age enclosure. Included within this suite of buildings was an

Figure 75. The Late Iron Age enclosure ditch at the St Loye's site infilled with Roman material following its abandonment. 2m scales. (© ECC)

Lyon ware lamps and cup

Central Gaulish colour-coated ware, from St Loye's

Lyon cup

Figure 76. Types of imported Gaulish and Lyon pottery found at the St Loye's settlement. (© Charlotte Coles)

aisled hall, a probable accommodation building, and workshops (Figure 77). The aisled hall had, in addition to deep and wide outer wall trenches, twinned pairs of internal post-pits intended to hold the massive posts necessary to support the roof of a building of at least two storeys in height (Figure 78). It bears a strong resemblance in plan to the aisled hall of the *fabrica* (metal-working shop) excavated at the legionary fortress at Exeter (Figure 79 and see above Figure 45). Quantities of hammer scale found in and around the aisled hall could point to iron smithing, although this could be residue from a nearby and more lightweight building for which there is also evidence. Perhaps the lightweight building (possibly just an open-walled roofed area) was a temporary smithy whilst the permanent structures awaited construction.

The aisled hall and the adjacent workshop buildings were fronted by what may have been an accommodation block or offices or a combination of both (Figure 77). It had an arrangement of rooms (Nos 1-4) which is similar to that of the non-cohort barracks provided for non-combatant craftsmen (*immunes*) working at the legionary *fabrica* at Exeter; it may have provided the living quarters for those employed in the adjacent buildings or workshops in the exact same manner. Larger rooms (Nos. 5 and 6) at the south-east end of the building were not divided and thus offered greater internal space. These rooms may have provided quarters for a more senior occupant such as an overseer of works. Other interpretations are of course possible.

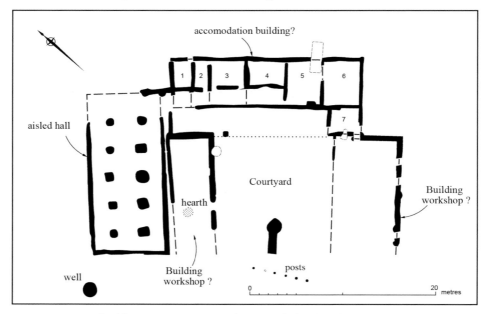

Figure 77. Roman buildings at St Loye's including an aisled hall and a probable accommodation building. Drawn by Tony Ives. (© ECC)

Figure 78. High-level photograph of the aisled hall at the St Loye's settlement site. Taken in summer, the deep shadows accentuate the depth of the foundations required for a building of this size. (© Jon Short, Aerialimage Highmast Photography and ECC)

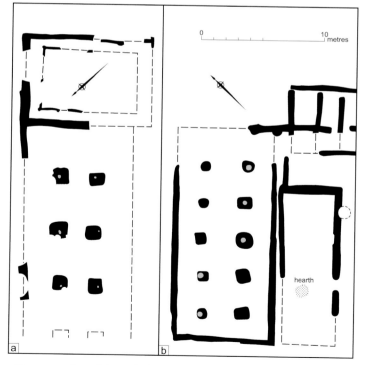

Figure 79. Plan of the aisled hall (*fabrica*) at the Exeter fortress (left) and the aisled hall building recorded at St Loye's (right) drawn to the same scale. Drawn by Tony Ives. (© ECC)

Figure 80. An amphora of the type which arrived in significant numbers at the St Loye's site.(© RAMM)

The extent of excavation at St Loye's did not extend as far as the Roman road frontage but some of those buildings just behind the road were found to have midden dumps of discarded broken pottery to their rear, including many sherds of both flagons and *amphorae*. Bidwell has pointed out that these significant amounts of *amphorae* sherds associated with the occupation of the site might indicate that part of its function was as a distribution centre for imported liquids. The distinctive two-handled *amphorae* (Figure 80) were used across the breadth of the Empire for the transportation of goods such as olive oil and wine, *defrutum* (wine sweetener) and *garum* (fish sauce), as well as fruits and olives. These products could have been decanted from the *amphorae* into smaller flagons for onward carriage. It is known that olive oil *amphorae* were typically single-use containers; once the oil was extracted, they could not be reused. This is because the interior of the *amphorae* became coated with a layer of solidified oil residue, which was difficult to remove. A giant midden comprising of nothing but broken olive oil *amphorae* still survives in Rome at Monte Testaccio. Are we seeing something similar at a very much-reduced magnitude at St Loye's?

The St Loye's settlement may then have served both as a manufacturing and commercial trading base under civilian control. Such transactions between the inhabitants of the settlement and the military authorities would have been conducted by merchant traders (*negotiatores*). The St Loye's settlement was probably receiving all manner of goods from Gaul and Spain on the Atlantic coast routes which were conducive to the Roman way of life. Animals were seemingly present at St Loye's, perhaps mules or other pack animals kept for the transportation of supplies by road. Evidence of stabling waste has come from a well infilled at the time of abandonment. Support for a supply role comes also from a metallurgy report which offers the opinion that thin lead

Figure 81. Top: the parallel double-ditch defences at St Loye's seen in section following excavation. (© ECC).

Right: the author 'trapped' with a 2m scale in a Punic ditch at Mermaid Yard, 1978. (© RAMM)

sheets found at the site are commonly believed to be 'baggage tags' attached to loads for identification; that may have been their purpose here.

A civilian settlement site such as St Loye's would not necessarily have been expected to possess military type defences of the kind seen in excavation, certainly not at this mid-first century date. Roadside settlements of the later second century were known to have been furnished with earthwork defences, but St Loye's was effectively closed down by around AD 75. The defences must therefore date to its main period of occupation which mirrors that of the fortress (*c*.AD 55-75). These defences comprised a rampart fronting two parallel ditches (Figure 81). Both ditches had similar average maximum widths of 3.6m and depths of 2.16m. However, whilst the outer ditch had a V-shaped profile, the inner ditch had an asymmetrical profile which identified it as a Punic ditch. A Punic ditch had asymmetric sides with a sloping inner face but a near vertical counter-face. It was designed to trick an enemy attacker into leaping the ditch onto a relatively gentle slope below the rampart. This could prove fatal. If forced back into the bottom of the ditch the attacker would have great difficulty in getting out. He would be faced with the task of climbing the initially hidden vertical counter face whilst exposing his back to those stationed with javelins positioned high above him on the rampart top. The deployment of substantial defensive measures at St Loye's is further discussed in Chapter 6.

The Topsham sites and a suspected barge-quay

If, as has been argued above, the St Loye's settlement was receiving goods from Gaul and Spain for onward distribution, then this presupposes the existence of a port or quayside somewhere on the Exe Estuary where the unloading of seaborne shipments of supplies could take place. The arguments in favour of just such an arrangement were put forward by Henderson who studied the question of the navigability of the Exe before the creation of weirs blocked the channel in the 13th century. He concluded that the difficulty of the passage caused by changing mud banks and the frequency of delays in times of drought or spate would have made river transport above Topsham very unreliable. He went on to state that: '*There must therefore have been an early Roman port on the estuary to handle supplies destined for the fortress at Exeter and the forts in its hinterland*'. This same conclusion had been arrived at by Ralegh Radford in the 1930s. Confidence in this proposal has been bolstered by the discovery of a number of sites in The Retreat area of Topsham, north-west of the modern town, where the M5 Motorway crosses the River Exe. Four open-ended strip buildings occupied in the period *c*. AD 55-75, were excavated at the Aldi supermarket site just north of the M5 crossing (Figure 82). The strip buildings were interpreted as warehouses forming part of a storage complex fronting onto the Roman road. Significantly, the excavators believed that these structures, were built by the Roman military but controlled or run by civilian traders who attached themselves to the legion in order to provide goods via trade. If this is correct, the site would have functioned in the same way as that suggested for the *vicus* settlement at St Loye's. The difference being that the warehouses suggest the storage of bulk provisions rather than the more delicate and perishable goods arriving at St Loye's.

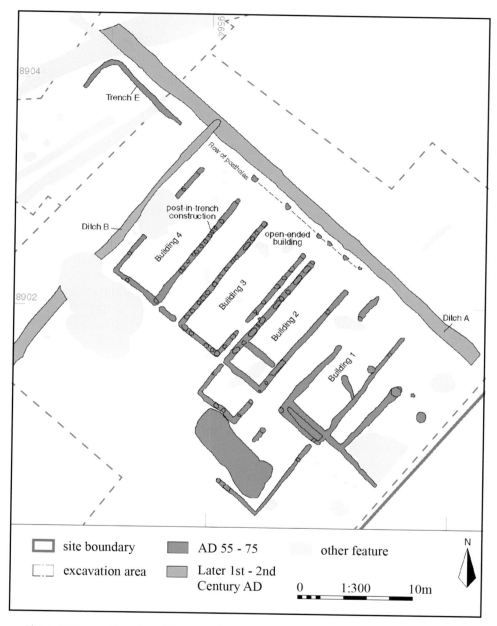

Figure 82. Excavation plan of Roman military-period open-ended strip buildings and later Roman features at the Aldi site, Topsham. (© Cotswold Archaeology)

A rectangular house of the military period was excavated in 1974 by Jarvis and Maxfield in advance of the M5 Motorway construction. It can be regarded as being part of the same settlement as the Aldi site just to its northwest.

A strong hint that the Roman military focus at Topsham was this riverside area slightly to the north-west of the modern town came from an observation that the line of the Roman road from Exeter seems to mirror the modern road to Topsham until it diverges from that alignment at a point somewhere north-west of the Aldi site. A ditch of the second century which ran in front of the open-ended warehouses may mark the edge of the road; this ditch replacing an earlier roadside ditch (Figure 82). If so the Roman road line, instead of heading into Topsham, would appear to head towards the river edge and Topsham School (see Figure 83 for location). It was at Topsham School that John Allan and Andrew Sage of Exeter Archaeology had found two parallel V-shaped defensive ditches in 2000. The ditches are undated but appear clearly defensive - having sharp V-shaped profiles. Originally thought to represent the rounded defensive corners of a fort on the banks of the River Exe, later work has shown this not to be the case and they are taking a more irregular course away from the river. They could be enclosing an area to the north-west but further investigation on this point will be necessary. John Allan did however draw attention to the previous recovery of relatively significant quantities of imported first century Roman material from sewerage works undertaken during the construction of The Retreat housing estate which lies just upriver from Topsham School between Exeter Road and the River Exe (Figure 83). Allan noted that the material contained more imported fine wares and exotic items than contemporary groups from the Exeter fortress. He observed that such finds assemblages are a typical feature of ports of all periods; the implication being that the pottery had travelled not far from its point of arrival. Within the recovered assemblage from 1933, were fragments of a first century glass vessel showing a chariot race in which Crescens was the victor over Pyramus (Figure 84). Other examples of this mould-blown glass beaker show Crescens holding aloft his champion's laurel wreath as he approaches the winning line. These vessels, which may have stylistic origins in Syria even if they were produced in the west of the Empire, are exceptional and few have survived. For one to have reached Topsham could be considered remarkable and its breakage no doubt much lamented at the time.

The question of the location of a Roman seaport and/or barge-quay, on the River Exe down river from Exeter, was addressed in 2022 by the current author and Stephen Kaye. Utilising a combination of historical and terrain-modelling data, the latter was able to calculate Relative Sea-Level (RSL) changes which had taken place between the mid-first century and the present day. This research confirmed that Roman sea-transports or river-barges could not have reached Exeter on the tide. Furthermore, the estimated tidal reach of the River Exe in the mid-first century AD allows limitations to be placed on the locations of both seaport and barge-quay facilities (Figure 83). For

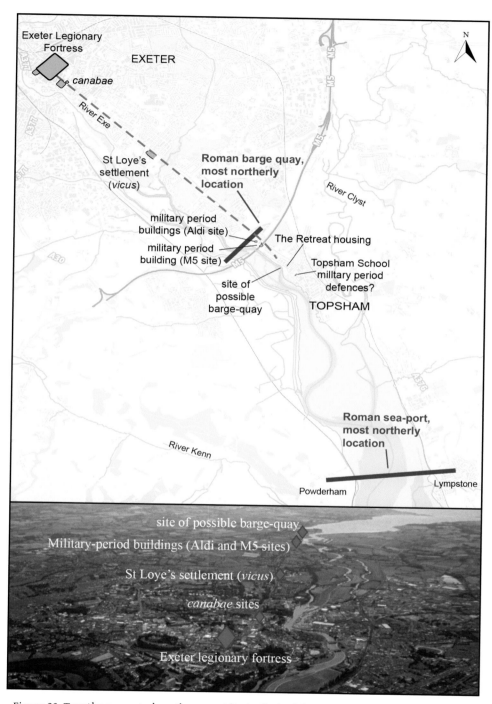

Figure 83. Top: the suggested northernmost limits for both barge-quay and sea-port locations on the River Exe estuary (© Stephen Kaye). Bottom: Aerial view of the estuary showing known and suspected Roman sites of the mid-first century AD

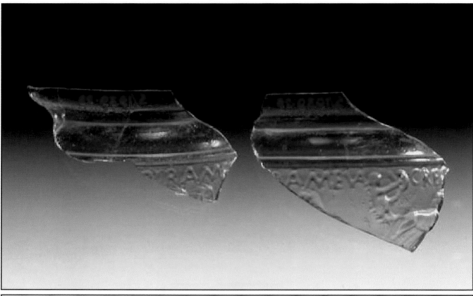

Figure 84. Top: fragments of an imported glass beaker of the first century depicting a chariot race between Crescens and Pyramus, Found at Topsham. Bottom: drawing as reconstructed from known examples. (© RAMM)

Figure 85. Left: detail of the prow of a 25m long, second century Roman river barge on display at the Museum Castellum Hoge Woerd, Holland. Right: a model of a Roman river barge of the same period. Photos: John Pamment Salvatore

example, for the purposes of discharging their cargo, seagoing transports could have progressed into the estuary no further than an imaginary line connecting Lympstone, on the east bank to Powderham on the west. Any establishment on the west bank would be extremely unlikely logistically, whilst no evidence exists of a Roman military period presence on the east bank of the estuary below Lympstone. If there was a seaport its location is unknown. Alternatively, and in the absence of a seaport, transhipment of goods from seagoing vessels to river-barges could have taken place on the lower reaches of the estuary. Flat-bottomed river-barges are known to have carried sizeable cargos on the River Rhine in the first and second centuries AD (Figure 85). River-barges may then have conveyed the transhipment up the Exe estuary to offload at a barge-quay.

A connected system

James Anderson has argued that the forts of North-East England were supplied primarily by road: '...*most supplies with production sites long distances away would have been shipped in by sea.......these materials would then have been carted or transported by pack animals over the Roman road system to each fort*'. It is conceivable that we are seeing the same process in operation on the Exe estuary. It may be seen as no coincidence that the greatest concentration of known mid-first century activity on the estuary, contemporary with the date of the legionary fortress, has been recorded on the east bank of the Exe, just below the location identified by Kaye as the northernmost limit for a barge-quay. The evidence presented could support a picture whereby goods were arriving from across the Channel to the mouth of the Exe estuary. From there they could be transhipped from seagoing vessels to barges; subsequently to be carried on the tide for off-loading at a quay somewhere at the head of the tidal estuary at Topsham. Given all of the above, the most likely position for a barge-quay would be somewhere between the Aldi site, just north of the M5 crossing, and Topsham School (Figure 83). If so, the scene at the quayside in the mid-first century AD might have looked something like that shown on Figure 86. Once ashore the various supplies could be stored in warehouses or taken immediately by road to the several different establishments now known to have been set up between Topsham and the fortress. At these sites the consignments could be broken down into smaller mixed loads to be sent on by pack animals to the fortress and to the forts further afield. Whilst no quayside remains at Topsham have yet come to light, this could be due to their loss resulting from a shifting of the course of the old deep water river channel over the past two millennia.

The occupants of the dependent sites

Figure 86. Imaginative illustration of a loading quay of the late-first century on the Corbulo Canal at *Forum Hadriani* (Voorburg-Arentsburg) in the Netherlands. If it existed, then a mid-first century AD barge-quay at Topsham may have looked similar. Illustration by Mikko Kriek. Copyright: Driessen and Besselsen

Paul Bidwell observed in 2021, that locally produced coarse pottery (known as Fortress Wares) was found in much greater quantities at the civilian sites of the *canabae* and the St Loye's *vicus*, rather than at the eponymous fortress itself. These wares were once thought to be closely associated with supply to the military, hence the name. Following Bidwell's later research however, the reverse is now true and the wares are considered to be produced and distributed largely by civilian potters for civilian consumption. Fortress Wares, although utilising local Devon clays, had some types with continental parallels (Figure 87). Vivien Swan considered that these locally produced versions were made by potters craft-trained in the region of north-west Burgundy, the Yonne, and the Loire valleys in Gaul. In addition to the potters, there must be every likelihood that the settlements at the *canabae,* St Loye's and Topsham were occupied by those who had travelled across from Gaul to take advantage of the trading opportunities which would naturally follow once the legion was in place at its Exeter fortress. Bidwell has suggested that the civilians involved in the logistics of army supply at the dependent sites would have been: '*.... negotiatores (merchants) and their agents, shippers and retailers – who would have been one part, and perhaps collectively, the wealthiest of the population in the extra-mural settlements*'. Could some of those wealthiest civilians have been the occupants of the buildings of the upper compound of the *canabae*? A coin hoard associated with those buildings (see below) hints at this, as does the recovery of a carrot amphora from the *canabae* (Figure 88). Carrot *amphorae* are believed to be used in the transportation of preserved fruits from the Middle East (most often dates) and they would have attracted a high price for their importation.

Figure 87. Fortress Ware jars (left) and a locally produced flagon (right). (© RAMM)

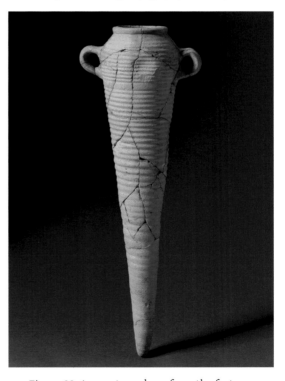

Figure 88. A carrot amphora from the fortress *canabae*. A type often used for the importation of fruits, such as dates, from the Eastern Mediterranean (© RAMM)

At a more mundane level, home grown production of crops may have been taking place in fields believed to be of early Roman date seen at the Wessex Close excavation at the Retreat area in Topsham. The fields were defined by ditches forming a regular ladder pattern, a type distinctively Roman and unlike the small irregular fields associated with contemporary Iron Age farmsteads. Perhaps these fields were being farmed also by an immigrant population who were part of the community living and trading with the Roman army at its legionary fortress from an early stage in the occupation of the area.

Period of occupation and abandonment

Study of the pottery from all of the dependent sites shows them to have been occupied at the same time as the fortress (*c*. AD 55-75).

At the *canabae*, the buildings of the upper compound appear to have been systematically demolished when no longer required. A hoard of coins, mostly those of Vespasian, with a date of deposition between *c*. AD 73-75 was dispersed within a layer of clay which was intended to seal off the demolition debris once the reusable materials had been removed. It is likely that the hoard had been secreted in the wall of one of the three buildings at the Valiant Soldier site (see above) and was not retrieved or evidently spotted when the walls were coming down. This discovery, together with pottery evidence, suggested to Paul Bidwell that the demolition programme took place at about the same time the legion was transferred to Caerleon in *c*. AD 75. The lower compound of the *canabae* appears to tell the same story with the drainage ditches, just outside its south-western corner, becoming infilled very shortly after AD 75. The infilling, which may have taken place as one event, included large amounts of discarded broken pottery. No pottery in the assemblage dated to later than *c*. AD 80. This would seem to confirm the picture of abandonment of the *canabae* by AD 75 or shortly thereafter. With the area of the upper compound vacated and cleared; the site became for a short while a prime spot for burial in a prominent location alongside the road to Topsham. Three cremations found in excavation at the Valiant Soldier site (see Figure 70 above) have been dated from their finds assemblage, and all are likely to have taken place in the period between *c*. AD 75-85.

The St Loye's site underwent a similar process of closure as the *canabae*. Wells were infilled and buildings at the rear of the complex were demolished around AD 75, although buildings closer to the road but outside the area available for excavation may have continued to function. The Punic ditch at St Loye's was backfilled with the rampart material pushed forward to seal it off (Figure 89). The open-ended warehouse buildings at the Aldi site, and the rectangular house at the 1974 M5 motorway site at Topsham, also provided evidence of having been closed down *c*. AD 75.

Figure 89. The Punic ditch at the St Loye's site showing the backfilled rampart material which appears light yellow due to the decayed organic content of the original turf blocks. 2m scale.
Photo: John Pamment Salvatore

Therefore, the pattern of contemporaneous occupation with that of the fortress, followed by a cessation of activity and a programme of deliberate demolition and closure at the time of the legionary transfer, can be shown to be a common feature of the dependent sites. The civilian camp followers and merchants reliant upon trade with the legion who occupied these settlements would have had no reason to stay following the departure of the legion. Consequently, most of them may have left for Caerleon to resume business there, with only a few perhaps choosing to stay to trade within the nascent town at Exeter.

Military establishments outside of the fortress

A defended site just beyond the north-east defences of the fortress was discovered at the Princesshay excavation of 2005 (see Figure 90 for location). Three parallel V-shaped ditches were excavated along with the post-pits of two interval towers. The inner ditch of the three was shallow and short-lived, being replaced by the two further ditches which were much deeper and wider. Pottery recovered from the initial ditch suggests that the establishment probably came

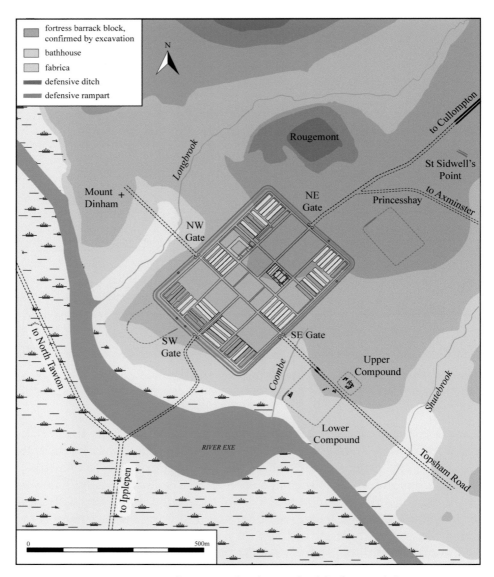

Figure 90. Location of sites immediately outside of the fortress defences.
(© Cotswold Archaeology). Re-drawn by David Gould

into existence a few years after the fortress was constructed. Paul Bidwell proposed that the location of these defences just outside of the fortress makes it likely that they were enclosing a small fort, possibly for auxiliary cavalry (Figure 91). It appears to have gone out of use at the same time as the departure of the legion in *c.* AD 75.

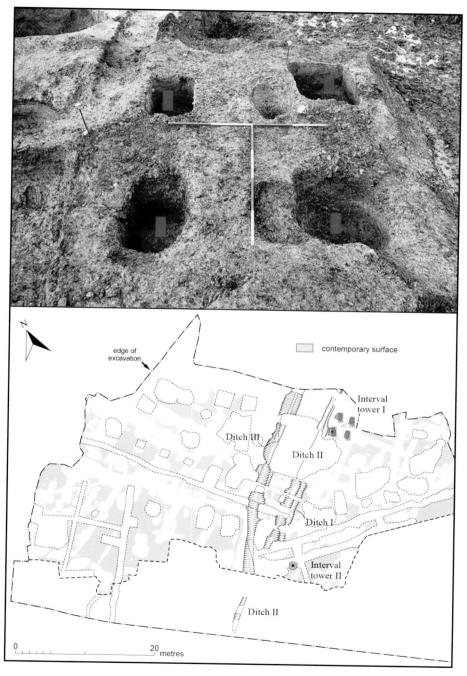

Figure 91. The defences of a possible fort site at Princesshay 2005. Top: photo of the interval tower post-pits; the position of the posts are marked with red dots. 2m scales. Bottom: plan of the defensive ditches (II and III) and the interval towers (© ECC)

Evidence of Roman military building activity was recorded at Mount Dinham, 150m north-west of the fortress, by Exeter Archaeology in 2007 (see Figure 90 for location). The remains of buildings of timber post-trench construction were found. The principal structure was a large timber building comprising an aisled hall, surrounded by small rooms and corridors, and a courtyard. The plan is not dissimilar to that of a *praetorium* (commander's house) found within a fortress. According to Bidwell, such buildings located outside of fortresses of exceptional strategic and administrative importance (which Exeter was), are suggested to have provided accommodation for high officials of the province. The building appears to have been occupied within the period *c*. AD 55-75.

Many of the above sites were excavated in the early decades of the 21st century. They have provided valuable additions to the previously known sites of the Roman military period in and around Exeter, which include the outlying fortlets at Stoke Hill, 3 km north of the fortress, and Ide, 5.5 km to the south-west. Both sites commanded extensive views over the lower Exe Valley and both could have acted as monitoring sites or possibly as signal stations. The fortlet at Ide, on the opposite side of the river from the fortress, could have provided early warning of any unwanted approach from the west.

Chapter 6

The fortress and its garrison at the time of the Boudican revolt

'....the dolabra (pickaxe) is the weapon with which to beat the enemy'.
Domitius Corbulo first century AD

The historical background

It is a matter of undisputed record that Boudica, a 'queen' (*dux femina* to the Romans) of the Iceni tribe of East Anglia, led a revolt against Roman rule which took a destructive path across mid-first century Roman Britain. The precise year in which the uprising took place (either AD 60 or 61), is uncertain, but many scholars, following Anthony Birley, now favour AD 60. The towns of Colchester, London and St Albans were destroyed. Boudica was eventually defeated at a site possibly somewhere in the Midlands, by the combined forces of the XIVth legion (*Legio XIV Gemina*) and veterans of the XXth legion (*Legio XX Valeria*). They were under the command of the Provincial Governor Suetonius Paulinus who had been on campaign in North Wales when he was forced to turn back in order to counter the threat from Boudica and her rebel army. Both units, the XIVth and the XXth, later received battle honours in recognition of their success with the suffix *Victrix* (Victorius) added to their standards (Figure 92). By way of contrast, the Second Augustan Legion appears to have been missing in action during the decisive battle. It is the Roman historian Tacitus who can shed some light on this matter. His account of the revolt and its aftermath leaves little room for doubt, that Poenius Postumus, the camp prefect of the Second Augustan Legion, had received orders to march the legion out from its base to join Paulinus, but had chosen not to do so. Tacitus does not elaborate

Figure 92. The legionary standards of *Legio XX* and *Legio XIV* (both carrying post-Boudican battle honours) and the standard of *Legio II Augusta* (author's collection)

on the reason why it was Postumus (the third in the chain of command of the legion) who received the order to march, rather than the legate (legionary commander) or his deputy. Nor does he name the base in question or explain why Postumus decided not to release the legionary cohorts at his disposal. He does tell us however, that the refusal of the order ultimately cost Postumus his life.

The dilemma of Poenius Postumus

In 1993, Graham Webster, in his book on Boudica, expressed some sympathy for Postumus taking the action (or rather the inaction) that he did. Webster believed that Postumus, whatever the local position, may have felt it imprudent to move any of his men as commanded, from the relative security at Exeter to a battle many days distant, where matters may already have been decided. It is possible to expand upon these ideas following some circumstantial archaeological evidence which emerged in 2014 as a result of the author's own research. Firstly, we have seen that the Exeter fortress is likely to have been constructed around AD 55, with AD 60 being at the upper end of the range of possibilities. We may believe with some confidence therefore, that it was indeed the Exeter fortress where Postumus was temporarily in charge of a significant number of cohorts which could potentially have made a difference to the outcome of the battle against Boudica. The absence from the fortress of the legate and his deputy (the *tribunus laticlavius*), might be explained if both senior officers were away campaigning in Wales alongside Paulinus, accompanied perhaps by only a small detachment of Second Augustan legionaries.

We have seen in Chapter 5 that there were several civilian settlements lying either side of a road which led from the head of the Exe Estuary to the fortress. (Figure 68). To take the legion away from Exeter would have left these civilian settlements at the mercy of a local native population, certainly not yet fully Romanised, possibly anti-Roman, and potentially emboldened by the success of Boudica as she took parts of the country by storm. If a related uprising in the South-West was feared by Postumus, then, on receiving the order to march, he would have been faced with a dilemma. He could either depart as instructed or stay and retain the fortress as a base from where the population of the nearby dependent settlement sites of civilian traders could be protected. The playing out of events according to Tacitus leads us to believe that Postumus must have chosen the latter course of action and, contrary to the orders, he did not take the Exeter cohorts up country to confront Boudica.

Defensive measures?

All of the above begs the question: if the legion stayed at Exeter then what was it doing? Significant in this respect is what had befallen Colchester at the hands of the Boudican rebels. Colchester (or *Camulodunum* as it was known to the Romans) had been the base for Legion XX following the invasion. When Legion XX left their fortress in AD 48 to move across country, the town which replaced it was given the status of a *colonia* (a self-governing settlement occupied by retired legionary soldiers and civilians). Before they departed, the legionaries had levelled the fortress defences; this proved to be a monumental error. When Boudica arrived some 12 years later, the town was burnt down and more easily overrun than would have been the case had the defences been retained and not dispensed with (Figure 93). Knowing this from reports, as seems likely, Postumus may have set about looking to prioritise the defences of those establishments outside of the fortress to ensure that Exeter and its dependent sites did not suffer the same fate as Colchester should there be a local uprising. His military career, which is likely to have been lengthy, had resulted in his appointment as a camp prefect; this made him well-suited for the role. A camp prefect was the senior officer responsible for the defences of the camp and its ordered layout of tents. At Exeter, Postumus would have overseen the upkeep of the defences and maintenance of the buildings. The fortress, as a military establishment, would have been furnished from the outset with a complete circuit of rampart and ditch defences, but it is unlikely that the contemporary commercial civilian sites outside of these defences had been equally well provided. If this was the case, then rather than sitting on their hands, the legionary cohorts may have

Figure 93. Archaeological evidence of fire-ravaged buildings at Colchester destroyed by Boudica
(author's collection)

been engaged by Postumus in ensuring that emergency defensive measures were taken to safeguard the sites and settlements beyond the gates of the fortress. He may have wished also to ensure the security and the continued use of the estuary barge-quay facility at Topsham. The legionaries will have been well-versed and highly trained in the art of ditch digging and rampart construction. We know that in peacetime the Roman army would practice the building of gateway defences and ditched earthworks; many examples of these exercises, including miniature practice camps, have been discovered across the Empire. Is there archaeological evidence which might support a picture whereby substantial but hurriedly constructed defensive measures were put in place in and around Exeter at some point during the Roman military period of *c.* AD 55-75?

The most compelling evidence which could be connected to an event seemingly requiring a significant military response, occurs at one of the *canabae* sites just beyond the fortress defences. We have seen in Chapter 5 that two compounds, believed to have been occupied and worked by civilian traders, have been identified just beyond the south-eastern gate of the fortress. At some stage during the life of the lower compound (*c.* 55-75 AD), its south-western corner was extended and defended by the construction of a ditch, a rampart and a wooden palisade. This evidence was recorded at the Lower Coombe Street site. At once it can be seen that the earthworks were of a very different nature and magnitude than anything previously marking the boundary of the establishment (see above Figure 71). A ditch with a V-shaped profile, with a surviving depth of 1.7m and a width of 2.7m was added; with a small channel allowing water to drain into the main drainage ditch alongside (Figure 94). It fronted a rampart which was relatively narrow - less than 3m wide in places. Where ditch and rampart were evidently found to be incompatible with the lower-lying and potentially marshy ground approaching the river's edge, the

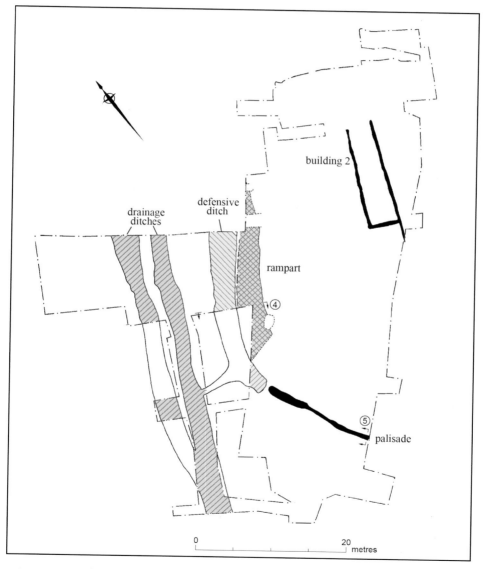

Figure 94. Detail of the defences and features at the south-west corner of the Lower Coombe Street site. Lower Compound of the *canabae*. Drawn by Tony Ives. (© ECC)

defensive duties were instead undertaken by a substantial wooden palisade (Figure 94). The trench dug to receive the posts for the palisade was over 1m deep which gives an indication that once in place the posts would have created a formidable barrier (Figure 95).

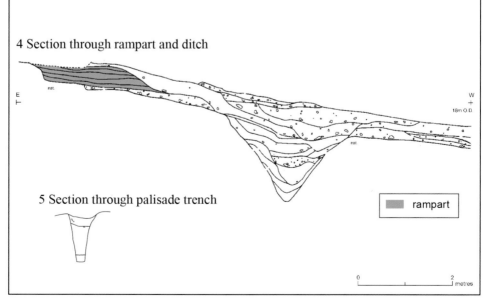

Figure 95. Top: V-shaped defensive ditch at Lower Coombe Street with 2m scale. Bottom: section drawings of the rampart, ditch, and palisade trench. (© ECC)

Therefore, what may be interpreted as defensive elements were introduced at the *canabae* at some time following its initial foundation, but they were of a lesser quality and therefore likely to be less durable than the ditch and rampart defences of the nearby fortress. For example, the rampart width of a little under 3m at Lower Coombe Street stands in contrast to the *c.* 4.6m rampart width accorded for the fortress defences. In addition, and significantly, no foundation pits for a timber corner tower were found within the south-western corner of the defences despite careful archaeological investigation. A corner tower, as part of a sequence of interval and corner towers, would be expected at this location within a conventional defensive circuit of a fort or fortress. The post-holes and massive post-pits required to support interval and corner towers leave an unmistakable archaeological signal in the ground (e.g. those seen on the fortress defences at the Friernhay Street site - see Figure 33 above). The defences at Lower Coombe Street do not therefore appear to conform in all respects with the defensive enclosures associated with permanent timber Roman military establishments. Rather, they resemble the defences of marching camps where a ditch and rampart would be put in place for a short period only, maybe only days or weeks if on campaign. Expediency, and the logistics of campaign, meant that temporary marching camps erected in potentially hostile country would not be furnished with labour-intensive timber buildings or interval towers.

Impressive defences were also found associated with the civilian (*vicus*) settlement of St Loye's (see above). Despite the most rigorous archaeological, open-area excavation, it was clear that no corner tower had ever existed on the south-western corner of the defences at the St Loye's site. Nor were there any traces of interval tower post-pits throughout the entire length of nearly 200m of the defensive circuit where examined. In this respect, the defences at St Loye's shared the same characteristics as those at the Lower Coombe Street *canabae* site; a measure of which is the absence of some features commonly found in the excavation of permanently occupied fort and fortress sites. This could be explained if, in the face of a perceived imminent threat, defensive measures were hurriedly put in place at an establishment whose occupation had never originally been intended to house military personnel.

Roman military-type defensive features were also found in advance of the construction of Exeter's replacement bus station in 2019 at the St Sidwell's Point site. These defences comprised a rampart fronted by a pair of parallel ditches. The inner ditch had a distinct Punic profile with a maximum width of 3.8m; it was 1.8m deep below the ground surface as revealed following the removal of modern deposits. The outer V-shaped ditch lay 3.5m beyond its companion and was 2.5m wide at its maximum width and 1.2m deep.

Neil Holbrook of Cotswold Archaeology noted that the ditch arrangement paralleled that found at St Loye's (i.e. an inner Punic ditch paired with an outer V-shaped ditch). Analysis of the pottery from the ditch fills at St Sidwell's Point shows that they were not infilled until the very late first or early second century, thus some decades after the departure of the legion. Holbrook went on to state that it was not out of the question that these defences might have been part of a linear earthwork that traversed the ridge between the river valleys of the Longbrook and the Shutebrook (Figure 90) and that they could have provided an additional level of defence for the fortress and its dependent installations. He concluded that: *'If the St Loye's defences were a response to a perceived insecurity, might also have been those at St Sidwell's Point?'*

A reasonable conclusion which might be drawn, is that an imminent threat did indeed give rise to emergency defensive measures being erected at sites which were considered to be vulnerable in and around the Exeter fortress. If so, the speedy nature of their construction could account for the absence of features which one would otherwise expect to find when excavating defences erected with the care and attention usually associated with permanent Roman forts and fortresses. It is worthy of comment that the ditched defences at both the Lower Coombe Street site and the St Loye's site were backfilled around AD 75 at the same time as the departure of the legion, whilst those at St Sidwell's Point remained open for some considerable period afterwards. This is not incompatible with the picture which has been presented above. The *canabae* site at Lower Coombe Street and the civilian settlement at St Loye's, were both purposefully levelled and closed down upon the departure of the legion when it was transferred to Caerleon around AD 75. Devoid of their civilian populations after AD 75 they would have no need of defences. Conversely, the emerging fledgling town at Exeter following the legionary departure would have held on to a population, even if it were not at the relatively high levels of before. Furthermore, the town was provided with a new Punic ditch forward of the retained fortress rampart, thus strengthening its defences rather than weakening them. This upgrade possibly took place just before the legion departed for Caerleon. Thus, the St Sidwell's Point defences, if put in place at the same time as those at St Loye's and Lower Coombe Street, could have been maintained as an additional outer line of defence for the new town for as long as the lesson of Colchester lived on in the memory. Only later when peace reigned would they slowly have become redundant before falling into disrepair.

The consequences

The attempted matching of archaeological data and historical events is a venture fraught with uncertainty. It is extremely unlikely that we will ever know with complete confidence whether any of the defensive works discussed above were undertaken on the instruction of Poenius Postumus. If they were, then Postumus may subsequently have felt vindicated given that Boudica was defeated without the aid of cohorts sent from Exeter. He would have ensured also, that the strategically valuable commercial assets remained in Roman control with its fortress, its dependent sites and their populations unscathed. Furthermore, he would have secured the on-going availability to Rome of the estuarine port facility at Topsham. Bidwell has even suggested that for several years after the suppression of the revolt, the supply lines that had passed through London and Colchester might well have been diverted to Topsham and Exeter whilst the towns destroyed by Boudica were being rebuilt and the normality of commerce in the South-East of Britain re-established. If this was the case any prominent trading role secured by Topsham may have been short-lived and Bidwell's 'several years' may have been as little as two. A wooden writing tablet recovered in London can be securely dated to AD 62. It records a contract between two Roman merchants in which 20 loads of provisions are to be sent from *Verulamium* (St Albans) to London by the middle of the following month. The month in question is November with the deadline for arrival of the goods being *idus Nouembres* (the ides [13th] of November). The year of AD 62 is confirmed by the opening declaration naming the Roman consuls in office at the time of the contract (much as legal documents in Britain prior to 1963 might carry a formal date in regnal years e.g. *In the 5th year of the reign of King Edward the VIIth* = 1905).The contract suggests that both these two cities destroyed by Boudica, had recovered rapidly from their devastation.

In any event, as Tacitus graphically relates, Poenius Postumus when he knew of the success of the men of the XIVth and XXth legions in the defeat of Boudica '....... *feeling that he had cheated his legion out of like glory and had contrary to all military usage disregarded the general's orders, threw himself on his sword'*. Postumus would have recognised that having disobeyed a direct military order from the governor of the province he had no choice but to make the ultimate sacrifice for his violation of military discipline. This extreme act of atonement could have taken place in front of the legionary standard and altar at the *principia* (headquarters building) beneath the heart of what is now modern-day Exeter at the junction of High Street and South Street.

Chapter 7

Exeter as a Roman town and *Civitas* Capital

'He (Agricola) would assist individuals and communities, to erect temples, market places and houses.....'

Tacitus *c*. AD 98

(on Gnaeus Julius Agricola, Governor of Britain AD 77/8-83/4)

The early town – a time of transition

Holbrook and Bidwell have argued that it is possible that Exeter had once been envisaged as a future *colonia* (a military settlement for retired veterans). This development had occurred at Colchester where the former legionary base achieved the status of a self-governing *colonia* inhabited by veterans from Legion *XX* and their dependents, alongside a civilian population. Such settlements, with their reserve of military expertise, could offer something of a safeguard against any latent native resentment following the invasion, although at Colchester this proved to be a false hope as the revolt of Boudica in AD 60 demonstrated. If Exeter had become a *colonia*, primarily for veterans of the Second Augustan Legion, then it may have taken a very different shape with many more of the legionary buildings retained. This did not happen and, as has been noted above, the garrison force of the Second Augustan Legion left Exeter for a new base in Caerleon around AD 75. Before they vacated the fortress it seems likely that, contrary to the decision taken at Colchester (where the defences were levelled upon the departure of the legion), at Exeter the defences were instead strengthened. This was accomplished by the infilling of the fortress ditch and its replacement, a little further out from the rampart, by a deeper ditch with a Punic profile (see above for an explanation of the subtleties of this type of ditch design). Where excavated at Rack Street, the Punic ditch

Figure 96. The defensive (Punic) ditch of the early town at Rack Street in 1977. 2m scale.
(© RAMM)

was 3.5m in depth and approximately 4m wide (Figure 96). Samian pottery recovered from the base of the infilled and subsequently redundant fortress ditch demonstrates that this upgrade of the defences is likely to have taken place around AD 75. Given the scale of work involved in enclosing what was to be the new civilian town, it is plausible that the whole exercise was carried out before the legionary redeployment and whilst the full manpower of the legion was still available. However, for the entire legion to have left Exeter may have been thought imprudent. The defences, no matter how sophisticated, would still require manning in the event of an attack (although a Punic ditch was almost certainly seen by the Romans primarily as a deterrent; their preference being to engage any hostile force on open ground where Roman discipline in rigid battle formation could be used to greatest effect). Paul Bidwell, writing in 2021, believed that a military presence, perhaps three legionary cohorts (about 1500 men) was retained at Exeter for the first years of the transition period from fortress to town. What appears to be evidence of continued occupation in barracks adjacent to the main south-west gate of the fortress was observed at the Friernhay Street site. Six ovens, shown to have been rebuilt after AD 75, perhaps served the six centuries of Cohort block H (Figure 97). In addition, a timber granary constructed post AD 75 just inside the north-east gate hinted at a military connection. A new smaller granary in this location might have been necessary to free up space for new town buildings in the centre of the

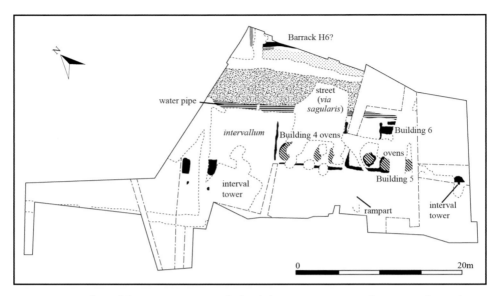

Figure 97. Plan of the post-AD 75 ovens behind the rampart at Friernhay Street. (© ECC)

former fortress by the demolition of the old granary. If so, there was a period of about a decade (between *c. 75 - c. 85*), or maybe a little more, when the town may have been under some form of military control with a *prefectus civitatis* (military administrator) overseeing the changeover to a civil administration. At some stage also during this interregnum, a reduction took place in the size of the bathhouse by making the *caldarium* (hot room) half of its original size. If Bidwell is correct, this reduction may reflect the smaller number of legionaries in residence after *c.* AD75.

A *civitas* capital (the early town and a new population)

Archaeological evidence shows that, after the departure of the legion, many of the fortress buildings were levelled and not converted for domestic use. On the other hand, some streets were retained, and others adapted and re-surfaced where necessary. The *via sagularis*, which ran around the inside of the defences, was maintained on at least three sides but possibly not on the north-east side where the new granary (see above) was built over it. With the legionary headquarters building no longer required, the former fortress streets of the *via praetoria and the via decumana* were linked up; this allowed a central axial street to run the length of the early town from the north-east gate to the south-west gate (Figure 98). With the introduction of some new street alignments, a traditional Roman town plan emerged based upon a grid system of *insulae* (blocks) created by a series of intersecting streets at right

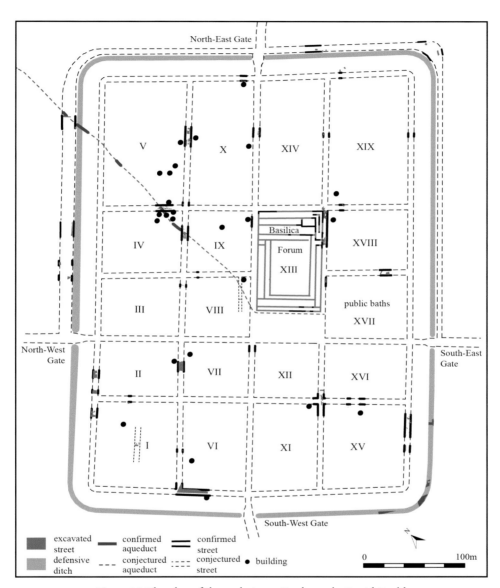

Figure 98. The plan of the early town. Re-drawn by David Gould

angles to one another. This was a form of town planning later adopted by many American cities, notably New York, in the early decades of the 19th century.

Exeter was only one of a number of towns that were being constituted as *civitates peregrinae* (provincial towns) during the decade AD 80-90. A *civitas* capital had a distinct legal status and acted as a centre of government and administration for a self-governing region whose boundaries were often but not exclusively based on those of the pre-Roman population. Given the topography of the South-West, with its long elongated peninsular to the west of Exeter, it is reasonable to believe that Exeter was the natural choice as a capital of the peoples who occupied what we would recognise today as the areas of Devon and Cornwall. Thus, Exeter became known in Roman times as *Isca Dumnoniorum*. *Isca* (deriving from the river Exe) prefixing *Dumnoniorum*; which together approximates to 'town of the Dumnonii on the river'.

Exactly when the status of a *civitas* capital was conferred upon Exeter is uncertain but AD 80 has emerged as an educated guess for the year of birth of the city. The year falls neatly into the middle of the governorship of Agricola who was credited by Tacitus with promoting building projects across the province (see quote at the head of this chapter). The foundation date of AD 80 is celebrated above the entrance to Exeter's Guildhall (Figure 99). The earliest inhabitants at the fledgling city of Exeter probably included those landowning members of the town council (the *ordo*) specifically appointed as magistrates or in other administrative roles befitting the status of the new town as a *civitas* capital. Joining them were perhaps a small number of those formerly resident at the dependent sites of the fortress, such as the St Loye's settlement, who chose not to follow the legion to Caerleon. The likelihood is that the total population at Exeter was far reduced following the legionary withdrawal.

Figure 99. The Exeter Guildhall celebrated 1900 years of the city (AD 80-1980). With legionary re-enactors from left, Oly Martin, Kevin Mills, and Kevin Orton (author's collection)

Bathhouse to Basilica and forum

It has been argued above that the military bathhouse could be viewed as a building exemplifying the physical manifestation of Roman power imposed upon the region during the first years of the occupation of the South-West. That same building was subsequently called upon to serve as a basilica which would be at the heart of the administrative town that was to follow the legionary departure. A basilica, often a building of some size and designed to impress, took the form of a long hall with one or more tribunals for magistrates. Behind the basilica hall there was usually a range of rooms containing the *tutela* (a shrine for the guardian deity of the town and the spirit of the place known as the *Genius Loci*) and the *curia* (the council chamber). Forward of the basilica, a business and commercial centre (forum) was arranged as a large courtyard surrounded by porticos on three sides, behind which lay ranges of shops and offices. Roman Exeter benefitted from having a ready-made and impressive building (the bathhouse) which could act in the role of a basilica, but it required a major conversion in order for it to fulfil that purpose. The formation of a basilica and forum for the new town thus required major works to the bathhouse and a reorganisation of the street plan around it. When completed, the entire complex of forum and basilica was to occupy an elongated *insula* (see *Insula* XIII on Figure 98). Holbrook and Bidwell have argued that this process of the physical transformation of the bathhouse into a basilica and the construction of the forum did not begin until *c*. AD 90.

The conversion works saw the demolition of the south-west wall of the bathhouse and its remaining furnace room. Internal walls were either demolished or adapted to fit with the new arrangement, whilst the infilling of the underfloor hypocaust system was achieved largely by the deliberate collapsing of the suspended floor. Two parallel walls about 9m apart were then built across the entire width of the former *caldarium* in order to create the front and rear walls of the basilica (Figure 100). Once in place, mortar floors were laid down for the various rooms of the new building. The remains of rooms behind the basilica hall included one room which the excavator Paul Bidwell confidently identified (see Figure 101) as the *curia* (council chamber). The forum was constructed by extending out from the demolished south-west wall of the bathhouse and across the former fortress street of the *via principalis*. The monumental stepped entrance into the new basilica from the forum was located in one of the very first trenches opened by the Exeter Museums Archaeological Field Unit in 1971 (Figure 102). Rows of covered stalls were probably set up in the forum selling a variety of goods and foodstuffs similar in appearance to a busy market day of our own times. Beyond the south-west boundary of the forum there was evidence of an open gravelled market place, probably for the trading of livestock.

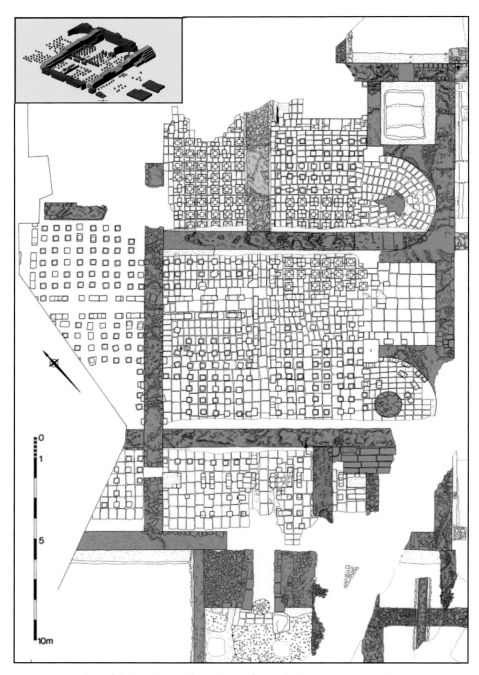

Figure 100. Plan of the basilica walls and steps (brown) shown overlaying the *caldarium* of the bathhouse. The original bathhouse walls are in blue (some were retained for the basilica building) (© ECC). Inset (top left) shows schematic version with the 'new' basilica walls shown in orange and bathhouse walls in red. (© RAMM)

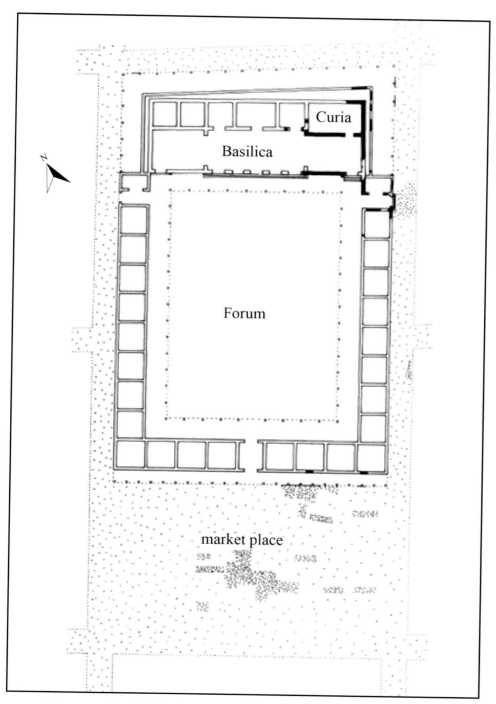

Figure 101. Plan of the basilica, forum and the external market place. (© RAMM)

Figure 102. The steps leading from the forum into the basilica. 30cm scale. (© RAMM).
Note the *pilae* tiles of the demolished bathhouse below the lowest step

Other features of the early town

Away from the town centre, occupation may not have been dense. For example, it was still possible, in the early years of the second century, for works across the north-western part of the town to be conducted apparently free from building constrictions. A project to bring in a water supply to the new town was achieved by tapping a source on the Longbrook Valley. Water was conveyed in an open wooden aqueduct running around the northern flank of Rougemont. It entered the town at the top of modern-day Paul Street where it crossed the defensive ditch of the town by means of a wooden launder supported on a timber bridge (Figure 98 for location). The wooden posts that supported the aqueduct as it crossed the town defences survived in waterlogged conditions having been driven into the silt and slumped clay which had accumulated in the ditch by the end of the first century (Figure 103). This suggests that the defensive ditch of the town was evidently no longer being properly maintained. The posts were proved by dendrochronology (tree-ring dating) to have been felled in the winter of AD 100-101 and they are likely to have been used for the bridge shortly after felling. The aqueduct then continued across the town by means of an open channel on apparently unoccupied land within *Insula* V (Figure 98). At least part of the channel was subsequently replaced by a wooden pipe and by the mid-second century houses overlay it, by which time the aqueduct must have been re-routed.

Figure 103. The remains of wooden posts which supported a bridge to carry the aqueduct launder where it crossed the partially infilled ditch of the town defences.1m scale. (© RAMM)

The new public baths, to replace the loss of the legionary bathhouse, are likely to have been constructed in the early years of the town's development. Tentative evidence suggests that they were sited within _Insula_ XVII (Figure 98). On the domestic front, evidence of the houses of the inhabitants of the early town at Exeter is scarce. A sequence of timber buildings at the Trichay Street site in _Insula_ IV predated a fire in the Hadrianic or early Antonine period (AD 117 to c. AD 150). Another building was

Figure 104. An _opus signinum_ (mortar) floor within a timber building of the early town in _Insula_ IV at the Trichay Street site. 2m scale. (© RAMM)

constructed at the Trichay Street site in the mid-second to early third century. Although constructed of timber this house was provided with a plain hardened mortar (*opus signinum*) floor (Figure 104). A Venus pipe-clay figurine, made in Gaul during the late first-second century, may have held a place in a personal or household shrine within a house in *Insula* VIII at this time. It was found by the author close to modern-day North Street in 1974. The Goddess; later stolen before going on display, has never been recovered (Figure 105).

Figure 105. Pipe-clay statuette of the goddess Venus probably from a household shine. Late first-early second century AD. (© RAMM)

Chapter 8

Late Roman Exeter

'The strength of the Empire lies within its people.'
attributed to the Emperor Constantine
by Eusebius writing in AD 337.

The Later town

In the second half of the second century a major decision was made to increase the size of the town from a modest 16.6ha to a much larger 37.5ha. The works to accomplish this expansion are likely to have taken place between AD 160 and 180. The redundant ditched defence of the early town was finally sealed off by the slighting of the old legionary rampart when the new expanded town defences were being erected. These new defences were initiated by the construction of an earth bank which incorporated within its bounds the volcanic hill and Roman quarry at Rougemont and the relatively lower-lying areas on the slope leading down towards the River Exe (Figure 106). The evidence suggests that the new boundary enclosed a great deal of open undeveloped space, but this was not unusual; other enclosed Roman towns at this time exhibited the same peculiarity. The earthwork rampart of the new circuit was about 1.5 to 2m in height and was constructed of mixed clays dug from the subsoil quarried for the creation of external ditches; it would have been faced with a timber or wattled revetment. Excavation by Exeter Archaeology at the South Gate found evidence of a timber gateway set back about 7m from the front of the rampart and contemporary timber gateways are likely to have been in place at the other three main entranceways into the town. With hindsight, the area taken in for the new town may have been over-ambitious – perhaps a statement of intent or urban aspiration which, as Holbrook has noted, was never quite fulfilled. Whatever the reason for their erection, the fresh defences were not to last for more than a few decades before there was a major upgrade from earthwork to stone.

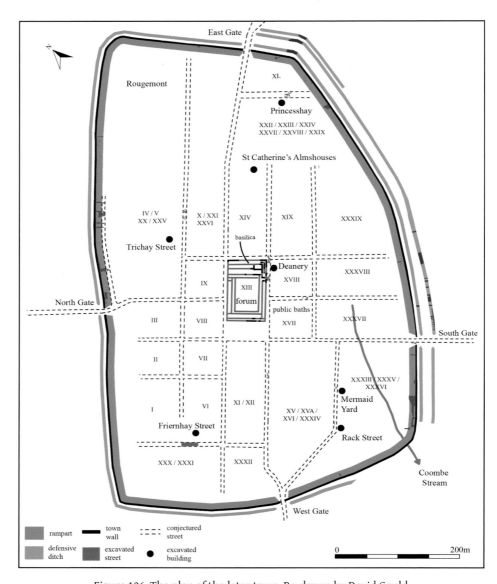

Figure 106. The plan of the later town. Re-drawn by David Gould

Exeter as a Roman city

When might it be legitimate to call Exeter a city rather than a town? It could be argued that its elevation as a *civitas* capital, perhaps by *c.* AD 80, would allow a justified use of the term at that early stage. In this book, both town and city have been employed with little qualification between the two terms. At least, perhaps in modern eyes, the 'city' claim has some greater substance when Exeter began to acquire those monumental buildings which characterised major

Roman urban centres (much the same way as the presence of a Cathedral was at one time a prerequisite of city status in Britain). Those buildings which one might expect to see in a Roman city include a basilica and forum, a temple, a theatre, an amphitheatre, and a circuit of walls. No temple has been found at Exeter, although a long boundary wall seen at the Friernhay Street site may have defined the *temenos* (the sacred enclosure around a temple). Likewise, no firm evidence has yet emerged of significant Roman structures such as a theatre or an amphitheatre. Could such evidence have evaded detection? The foundations for a sizeable Roman circus for chariot racing remained hidden beyond the walls of Colchester until 2004 when they were uncovered on the site of a new development. Colchester however, had, since the invasion, been one of the predominant Roman cities of the province, and as a *colonia* would have been home to large numbers of retired soldiers and their dependents. Perhaps Exeter had an insufficient Romanised and wealthy population which could support extravagant buildings constructed for public amusement.

Third and fourth century developments

A rebuilding or modification of the public baths took place just either side of AD 200 around the same time that Britain was divided into two provinces: Britannia Superior and Britannia Inferior. Exeter was within Britannia Superior which

Figure 107. Excavation at North Gate showing the original town rampart and later stone wall and its accompanying raised bank

had its provincial capital in London. In the early decades of the third century, Exeter already possessed its re-modelled basilica and forum and a street plan in the form of a grid with an administrative building at its centre; but with the addition of a city wall we have something new which provides a visible and tangible link to Rome. Excavation across the line of the wall demonstrated that the front of the earlier earth rampart surrounding the city had been cut away towards the end of the second century and replaced by faced stone walling with a higher bank raised behind the wall (Figure 107). The wall of this date, which stood upon a plinth, survives at a few certain locations on the much-rebuilt circuit. One of the best sections is at Quay Lane on the south-east side (Figure 108). The stone gateways into the city may have been impressive. This was certainly the case at the South Gate where Henderson further investigated the excavation work which had been carried out between 1989-1994 by Exeter Archaeology (see Figure 106 for location). From the information recovered, coupled with the 1964 observations by Lady Fox, Henderson was able to offer a conjectural reconstruction drawing of the South Gate as it would have appeared in the third century (Figure 109). From this work, and based upon the tower foundations exposed in excavation, the outline of the third century gate tower on the western side (together with the line of the city wall), could be marked out with zig-zag paving (Figure 110). The wall on the relatively level north-east and south-east sides of the city was fronted by at least two ditches and, where excavation took place at Princesshay in 2005, it was found that there were three (see Figure 106). We can be reasonably certain therefore, that by the early decades of the third century, Exeter had acquired a number of classical features to identify it unmistakeably as a Roman city not dissimilar to those found in Roman Gaul; albeit not quite as grand or well-appointed as those closer to the Mediterranean heartlands of the Empire,

Although a number of the streets of the early town were retained, there was some realignment of the street system from the early third century onwards. There appeared to be no great impetus to extend the building programme out to the expanded boundary of the city; peripheral areas remained seemingly vacant although streets were set out as if to receive buildings (see Figure 106). In the city centre however, a masonry house had already been constructed in the late second century in *Insula* XVIII opposite the south-eastern side of the basilica. The building is the earliest known masonry house in Exeter. Some of its second century walls were later incorporated into a new house constructed before *c.* AD 250.

The basilica itself underwent a major phase of reconstruction at some point after *c.* AD 220. The evidence suggests a beginning of this work in the second and third quarters of the third century, probably due to fabric failures of the original

Figure 108. Roman City Wall at Quay Lane. Roman facework of volcanic blocks to full height on the original plinth. Later works have reduced the original ground level leaving the plinth exposed; this was underpinned in the 19th century with rough stonework including Breccia blocks (© ECC)

Figure 109. A conjectural reconstruction drawing of the early third century South Gate according to C.G. Henderson. Drawn by Piran Bishop. (© RAMM)

Figure 110. Top: exposed foundations of the western tower of the South Gate with 25cm scale.
(© RAMM). Bottom: drone image of the same tower marked out by zig-zag tiles in South Street.
(© Jonathan Newell)

bathhouse walls. Floors which had been at different levels in the basilica were made uniform and the probably defective south-east end wall was demolished and made way for a new extension. The extension increased the length of the room identified as the council chamber. Together with contemporary improvements to the forum, the works would appear to demonstrate a healthy administration and economy for the city at that period.

A late third century town house which spread across a wide area just inside the walls appeared as a result of the extensive redevelopment of the Princesshay shopping precinct which took place in 2005-6. Exeter Archaeology revealed the plan of various buildings of the town house which had a sprawling, less concentrated layout than those nearer to the basilica. The westernmost building of the house had a private bathing suite; the remains of a channelled hypocaust system was recorded, along with the robbed-out foundation trenches of a plunge bath. The house had been built over the street which demarcated *Insula* XL on Figure 106. The period of occupation of the house was lengthy and it may not have gone out of use until the late fourth century. The recovery of 500 loose *tesserae* at the site suggests that the house had at least one mosaic.

Only eight mosaics are known from Exeter. One of the best surviving examples to date was found in a town house of the late third or early fourth century at St. Catherine's Alms Houses (*Insula* XIV), excavated by Mark Knight in 1988 (Figure 111). Another, although badly damaged, was excavated by the author and Colin Tracey in the excavated rooms of a town house of the first half of the third century. Located in front of the Cathedral to the north-east of the Deanery in Insula XVIII (see Figure 106), this was a substantial rebuild of the late second century town house which preceded it. Holbrook observed that the recovered Exeter mosaics displayed a generally lower standard of workmanship than those seen in the towns further to the east.

Away from the heart of the city at a site at Rack Street, three rectangular buildings were identified alongside a street in the south-east quadrant within *Insula* XXXIII (Figure 106 for location). Originally constructed of timber they were later rebuilt in stone (see below). One of the buildings contained an oven, almost certainly used for baking and possibly the cause of a fire which destroyed the timber phase. The oven was well preserved with a plank-lined ash pit floored with ceramic tiles (Figure 112) .

Events a long way from Exeter dominated the final years of the third century and the first decades of the fourth. The admiral of the Roman Channel fleet, Carausius, declared himself Emperor of Britain and Northern Gaul in AD 287. He began minting his own coinage, some of which reached Exeter and was lost here.

Figure 111. Town house mosaic of the late-third or early-fourth century subsided into the earlier legionary fortress ditch at St Catherine's Almshouses. (© RAMM)

In AD 293, Carausius was assassinated by his treasurer, Allectus. In AD 296, Rome recaptured Britain and Allectus was killed in battle. If either Carausius or Allectus had supporters in Exeter then confiscation of their property could have occurred with the restoration of official Imperial rule, but such matters remain beyond archaeological detection. An administrative reform at about the same time saw Britain further sub-divided, this time into four provinces. Exeter was in Britannia Prima which had a new provincial capital at Cirencester.

The Emperor of the East, Diocletian, had divided the Empire into east and west around the turn of the fourth century but this division was short-lived and the Empire was reunited with the coming of Constantine (The Great). It was Constantine who had succeeded

Figure 112. An oven of the late-third to early-fourth century in a bakehouse building at Rack Street. 1m scale. (© RAMM)

his father Constantius who had been the Emperor of the West and who died at York in AD 306. The acceptance of Christianity as a recognised religion of the Empire by Constantine in AD 313 was to prove to be of the highest significance for the religion and aided its spread across the known world. At least one Exeter citizen appears to have been an adherent. The Christian chi-rho symbol (the first two letters of Christ's name in Greek) was found scratched into a fourth century potsherd found in excavations at the top of South Street (Figure 113).

At the Guildhall site of Trichay Street a masonry courtyard townhouse of probable mid-fourth century date was introduced (see Figure 106). It was built on a much grander scale than anything previously on the site and it was furnished with corridor mosaic pavements (Figure 114). A street which had survived from the fortress period and which had once demarcated a division between *Insula* IV and *Insula* V was swept away in order to accommodate the building programme. Some commentators have described these houses with associated ranges of outbuildings, barns, and stock enclosures, as 'urban villas',

Figure 113. A Christian Chi-Rho symbol incised onto a pot sherd (probably of the fourth century). Found in South Street by Lady Fox. (© RAMM)

referencing the suite of buildings, both domestic and agricultural, which one might find at a contemporary Roman villa in the countryside. Although boasting mosaic pavements and a small heated bathhouse, the courtyard house was in a somewhat rustic setting. Associated with it was a stockyard and some ditched enclosures to the north-west, possibly for holding cattle prior to slaughter. Butchered cattle bones were recovered from the infill of the enclosure ditches. The stockyard had accumulated a trampled soil over time resulting from the movement of animals. Finds from the stockyard soil date its use to the mid-to-late fourth century. This activity, more suited perhaps to a rural environment and taking place so close to the centre, prompted Holbrook to suggest that the city was rather a dirty and muddy place in the late Roman period.

The owner of the Trichay Street courtyard house may have had a distinguished ancestor. A miniature portrait head was found amongst demolition rubble of the late fourth century in an enclosure close to the house (Figure 115). Expertly fashioned by a Mediterranean sculptor in white marble, it has stylistic characteristics of the late first century and depicts an elderly man, bald on the crown of the head, and with facial creases. It may have been curated and kept as a memorial bust in a private shrine within the house, just as we

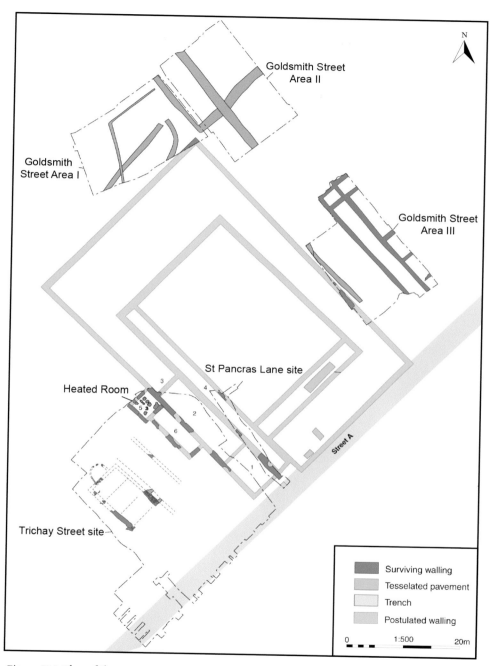

Figure 114. Plan of the Late-Roman townhouse, *Insula* IV, Trichay Street. Drawn by David Gould.
(© Cotswold Archaeology)

Figure 115. Sculptured marble head of a man. Stylistically of late-first century date it may have been curated as a memorial bust set up in a private house. (© RAMM)

Figure 116. Imaginative drawing of a mid-fourth century mother and daughter spinning wool at an Exeter town house. (© Graham Sumner)

might today keep photographs of grandparents on the mantlepiece in the living room. The owner of the house in the fourth century could be described as an urban farmer and he was probably fully self-sufficient. His extended *familia* would include not only his immediate family members but freedmen and slaves who would have undertaken the bulk of the domestic tasks and the animal husbandry. His wife and any daughters, in the Roman tradition, would have been responsible for the spinning of wool and the fashioning of clothes which was considered by the Romans to be a worthy womanly occupation with no loss of social status attached to the task (Figure 116). The Roman historian Suetonius tells us that even the Emperor Augustus '......*wore house clothes woven and sewn for him by his wife Livia or one of his granddaughters*'.

The timber houses (see above) at Rack Street were rebuilt in stone in the early-mid fourth century. When excavation took place it was found that the walls of the replacement buildings had been largely robbed of their stone, leaving only some river cobble foundations and the occasional volcanic trap in place. However, the neat robber-trenches left clear indications of where the buildings had once stood (Figure 117). One of these buildings (that on the far right of Figure 117) appears to have replicated the bakehouse purpose of its timber predecessor. It was furnished with hearths and

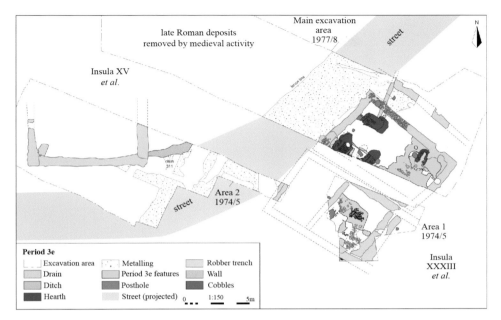

Figure 117. A plan of the stone buildings (including a bakehouse) flanking a Late Roman street at the Rack Street site. Drawn by David Gould. (© Cotswold Archaeology)

ovens. The buildings lay alongside a street which had probably led to the West Gate and which was recorded also at a site at Mermaid yard to the north-east (Figure 106). On the basis of coin evidence, the street continued to be in use after *c.* AD 350 but perhaps not for long afterwards (Figure 118). A further building, also robbed of its stone, stood on the opposite side of the road. The buildings were probably demolished shortly after the middle of the fourth century and occupation appears to end here, as it did in the suburbs beyond the South Gate, by *c.* AD 360. Following this there is seemingly a contraction of occupation back towards the core of the city and the central *insulae* around the forum.

An inhumation cemetery for the Roman city has so far eluded detection. With burial precluded by law within the walls, internments may have taken place outside the city on three of its four sides (the fourth side being disregarded due to the River Exe). Whilst human bone can survive well in the clay soils of the city centre they do not do so in the acidic soil conditions beyond and no skeletal remains are therefore available for dating purposes. This might account for the absence of burial remains when the 18th and 19th century suburbs of Exeter were being constructed; perhaps the 'empty' graves were simply not observed. This may have been the case at St Davids in the area around St Michael's Church and Haldon Road to the north of the city which was developed for housing from the mid-19th century. The remains of a late Roman mausoleum were found at Dinham Road in the same area to the north of the city in a modern excavation.

Figure 118. Late Roman street at Mermaid Yard 1978. Full width cut by later features. 2m scales.
(© RAMM)

This monument is unlikely to have stood alone. Perhaps it was surrounded by less ostentatious unmarked graves which were not recognised for the reasons stated above. Dispersed graves of the later Roman period have been recorded on the edges of the settlement areas at St Loye's and at Topsham. None of these burials produced human remains, although coffin nails were often present and two of the St Loye's burials had hobnails in the position where the feet had most likely been placed.

A conjectural reconstruction of the city of Exeter as it may have looked around AD 350 was produced in 1980 (Figure 119). This is likely to be over optimistic in the density of the occupation shown but does give some flavour of the appearance of the city before its expansion beyond the walls many centuries later and the dominant location of the basilica and forum at its heart is abundantly clear. However, there is no evidence for the 'watergate' shown on the south-eastern corner of the wall in this reconstruction.

Figure 119. Imaginative view of the City of Exeter as it may have looked *circa* AD 350. (© RAMM). Volcanic stone for the city's buildings was quarried from the Rougemont quarries (shown top and right of centre on the image)

Topsham in the third and fourth centuries AD

Topsham (or rather the area north-west of the modern town) is likely to have supported a thriving Roman population into the late third century and beyond. A settlement based around quay facilities which were probably in place from the mid-first century seems likely. Holbrook has suggested that an area of occupation in the order of 20-25ha may have lain alongside the estuary foreshore extending from the M5 crossing south-eastwards towards Topsham School, and inland on both sides of the Roman road. A stone building of this settlement with an origin in the late second century AD, was excavated by AC Archaeology in 2015 at Wessex Close to the north-west of Topsham School. The building, of riverworn cobble foundations, presented the plan of an aisled hall with a double-height nave and narrow single story side aisles which faced the river and the road to its south-west (Figure 120). The building was regarded by its excavators as multi-purpose, incorporating aspects of a residence and a warehouse. There was evidence also, from the ovens located in the front aisle, of crop processing and salted fish-sauce production. The rear aisle was perhaps a storage area, scatters of amphora were found there. The building

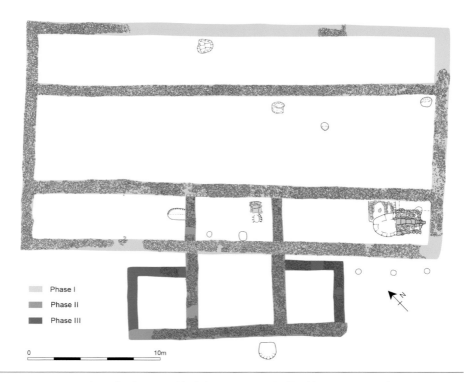

Phase I

Phase II

Phase III

0   10m

Figure 120. Top: photo (looking south) of the masonry aisled building at Wessex Close, Topsham
with 2m scales. Bottom: plan of the same building. (© AC Archaeology)

appears to have been long-lived, it acquired a rather grand portico entrance and only went out of use perhaps towards the end of the third century. A stone building, with riverworn cobble foundations but smaller than the Wessex Close example, was found in 1938 at Yarde's Field on the site of the Topsham Rugby Club. This building, thought to be of fourth century date, was at some distance away from the river and seemingly on the periphery of the settlement. It contained two ovens and the recovery of quern stones used for milling flour led to its interpretation as a bakery. There is no reason to believe that Roman Topsham had not prospered throughout the third and fourth centuries in the same manner as Exeter.

Chapter 9

The end of Roman Exeter and the beginning of a new story

' The lights appear to go out early'
A. Brown and S. Moorhead 2021

Roman and Saxon historical sources appear to suggest a breakdown in the Roman administration in Britain, certainly by the first decade of the fifth century AD. A date of 409 or 410, when the province is cautioned by the Emperor Honorius to look to its own defences, has traditionally been taken to mark the end of Britain as part of the Roman Empire. Is there anything which might assist in answering the question of when Exeter ceased to be a functioning Roman *civitas* capital? One indication might be seen in the coin supply to the city. It is reasonable to believe that Exeter, being an urban centre somewhat isolated geographically in the far west of the province, would feel the effects of any destabilisation of the economy at a relatively early stage.

Coin supply as evidence of decline

If we examine the coin evidence we find that no coins of the Emperor Honorius (who reigned from AD 393-423) are known from Exeter, and only one single coin of Theodosius I (AD 379-395) has so far been recovered. A study of coin loss at Exeter by Brown and Moorhead found that the city suffered a decline in coin loss from AD 348-378 with an almost total collapse in the importation of new coinage after AD 378. This was in stark contrast to contemporary evidence from other Roman towns not too far distant to the east, such as Ilchester and Cirencester, a finding which prompted Brown and Moorhead to make the comment seen above at the head of this chapter. We might see this as a signal that Exeter was in a spiral of economic and related administrative decline some decades before the end of the fourth century. This view is reinforced by Brown and Moorhead's questioning of the role of Exeter in these two important spheres given that market activity indicated by coin loss appears to be stronger outside of Exeter, particularly along the south coast of Devon, rather than at Exeter itself. They state that the evidence suggests that: '*....contact between Roman officials and traders with the local population was made at a more local level'.*

The end and a new beginning

If the Roman State had indeed turned away from Exeter by the end of the fourth century, then it had little claim to be regarded as a Roman city. With its administrative status eroded away, one can imagine that Exeter became a *civitas* capital in name only by the last quarter of the fourth century. How long urban life continued to limp on in Exeter in the last decades of the fourth century is a matter of conjecture. The courtyard townhouse at Trichay Street (see above) appears to have been demolished in the late fourth century. Was there an exodus to the countryside by the remaining population where, as Brown and Moorhead seem to suggest, there may have been greater opportunity in a rural way of life? Evidence of the material culture of the immediate post-Roman period in Devon is hard to come by. Imports of fifth to sixth century imported Mediterranean and North African tablewares turn up at coastal sites such as Bantham in South Devon, but none at Exeter. Otherwise, Devon is aceramic in contrast to Cornwall where a pottery tradition continued. A post-Roman cemetery discovered by Exeter Archaeology at Kenn some 7.2km south of Exeter provided evidence of 111 graves within the area investigated, but bone survival was very poor. The ordering of the graves in rows suggested a managed cemetery characteristic of the post-Roman period. There were five ditched or walled burial enclosures similar in ground plan to that found at Dinham Road in Exeter (see above). Radiocarbon dates recovered give earliest probable dates of the early fifth century. Bidwell, who analysed the pottery from the layers through which the graves were cut, found that it dated to the second half of the fourth century; the assemblage indicated a high-status site in the vicinity. The excavators concluded that the cemetery may possibly have had an origin in the late fourth century.

Whatever became of Exeter's Romano-British inhabitants it can reasonably be deduced that once the buildings were no longer fully maintained they will have fallen into disrepair rapidly. Wooden roofing timbers will soon rot away in the wet South-Western climate and vegetation will begin to take hold if left unchecked. Many historic towns with Roman origins have been observed in excavation to have accumulated so-called 'dark soil' immediately above the latest Roman occupation levels and this is true of Exeter. The deposition process for this phenomenon is not however clearly understood – the dark earths may not necessarily build up in the same way in every town, nor are they always dark in colour despite the name. Dark earth deposition has been recorded in Exeter at a number of different sites where excavation has exposed the remains of late Roman buildings. Subsequent agricultural activity and disturbance often makes it impossible to estimate with any degree of accuracy when the accumulation of dark earth took place. Where subsequent cultivation has occurred much later material from the medieval period tends to become mixed in with the Roman material. A significant depth of post-Roman dark soil was exposed in 2023 in an excavation at a location close to the Roman core of the city just to the north-east of the basilica in *Insula* XIX. The dark soil, here brown in colour, was located as an occupation deposit immediately above the mortar floor of a room within a late Roman town house. Richard Macphail, who studied this deposit, determined, from the traces of hammer scale recovered, that the population which post-dated the Roman city was engaged in iron working. Small cooked fish bones found in the soil shows that they were consuming fish. In this central location at least, it seems there was not the full abandonment which would have resulted in collapsed building material covering the mortar floor, rather than the occupation deposit found.

The earliest dated post-Roman evidence at Exeter comes from two burials found immediately to the west of the Norman Cathedral. Both were radiocarbon dated to the fifth to seventh centuries. Given that Roman law forbade burial within the confines of a town or city then any vestige of a Roman administration had clearly gone when those internments took place. Thus, our story of Roman Exeter must have ended before those two citizens were laid into the ground, but the wide date range provided by their radiocarbon results does not greatly assist us.

Figure 121. The foundations of a Roman town house wall survived beneath the medieval Cathedral cloister walls. The medieval wall rides up over the Roman wall on a different alignment. 0.5m scale. (© AC Archaeology)

There must however, in addition to the walls, have been some recognisable remains of the Roman city which greeted the arrival of the Saxons in the seventh century. For example, the lower courses of the wall of a Roman town house had survived for many centuries to be incorporated into the cloister wall foundations of the Norman Cathedral. The cloister wall, on a different alignment to its Roman predecessor, can be seen following exposure in excavation to have ridden up over the Roman work (Figure 121).

Final Thoughts

'All right, but apart from the sanitation, the medicine, education, wine, public order, irrigation, roads, a fresh water system and public health, what have the Romans ever done for us?'

Reg of Judea....... AD 33
(Monty Python's Life of Brian 1979)

Following the invasion of Britain, the imposition of a Roman administration based on a monetised economy, together with the creation of towns and cities and the introduction of new agricultural practices, transformed society and the country in a fundamental way. Certainly, many of our major British cities and towns would look rather different from the way they do today had it not been for Roman urban town planning - some of them may not have come into existence at all. When we walk down Fore Street towards the River Exe we are following literally in the steps of those legionaries whom, at a date only twenty years or so after the crucifixion of Christ, would have walked from the gate of the fortress down to the river crossing. Without them there is no guarantee that a Roman settlement, or indeed one of a later period, would have grown into the city which we now call Exeter.

That we knew nothing of the presence of a Roman legionary fortress beneath the streets of the modern city until the early 1970s may now seem remarkable looking back. With some city centre areas yet to be redeveloped at the time of writing, there remains the possibility of yet further Roman discoveries. Perhaps the greatest potential however now resides beyond the city walls. With growing recognition that defences may have been put in place in response to a perceived threat, perhaps at the time of the Boudican revolt, there is a distinct possibility that defensive earthwork and ditch systems of the Roman military period are more extensive than has so far been revealed. Furthermore, the intriguing Roman military building complex at Mount Dinham, has yet to be fully investigated and understood. Elsewhere, Roman Topsham appears to have much more to tell us of life and commerce there during what could be up to four centuries of trading. All of this will be a task for future archaeologists.

Lastly, we should never forget the people of Roman Exeter, a recognised Roman city holding its own on the extreme western edge of the Empire. A city which today still boasts its standing Roman walls and something of its Roman street plan. The birthplace of the city survives too, albeit hidden

Figure 122. The Spire of the demolished St Mary Major Church retained on Cathedral Close and located above the Roman bathhouse and basilica remains. Photo: John Pamment Salvatore.

underground. The cross from atop the spire of the former St Mary Major church in Cathedral Close marks the spot nearby where the basilica steps still lie below the grass (Figure 122). This is where the city's Roman forefathers would once have entered the basilica to hold council and to discuss the business of the day. Lady Fox, on seeing the steps revealed in one of the earliest excavation trenches cut by the archaeological unit she had been instrumental in creating, later stated: '*I shall long remember seeing in one of the first cuttings the monumental flight of steps which subsequently proved to belong to Isca's basilica*'. It is fitting perhaps, that Lady Fox should provide that final reflection on Exeter's remarkable Roman heritage.

Acknowledgements

I am forever indebted to Chris Henderson who led me through the archaeological journey of discovery at Exeter whilst Paul Bidwell was, throughout the course of 50 years, always ready to discuss latest ideas and thoughts on Roman Exeter.

David Gould has provided the expertise for the work on the production of all plans and illustrations with great patience on his part. During the preparation of the text for this book Henrietta Quinnell has provided invaluable support, comment and advice, as has John Allan, Stephen Kaye and Peter Marsden. Copy editing was undertaken by Phil Newman. My thanks to all of them. I am most grateful to Steve Rippon of the University of Exeter and Neil Holbrook of Cotswold Archaeology for their generous provision of material from their 2021 volumes: *Exeter: A Place in time*. Archive and source material was provided by Tom Cadbury, Assistant Curator of the Royal Albert Memorial Museum (RAMM) and the staff of the South West Heritage Centre, Exeter, for which many thanks. I would also like to thank the librarian and the staff of the Devon and Exeter Institution.

The St Loye's site, which features heavily in this book, would not have featured had it not been for the diligence of Andrew Pye, former Principal Officer (Heritage) of Exeter City Council. He led the way in securing funding and ensuring that open area excavation was conducted by Exeter Archaeology (and subsequently by AC Archaeology). prior to development. My thanks to Andrew, and Exeter City Council.

Those who have read and commented upon sections of this book or who have otherwise contributed towards its improvement and publication include Frances Griffith, Bill Horner, Denise Allen, Tim Gent, Andy and Kate Hannan,

Nigel Cheffers-Heard, Paula Fernley and Colin Barrington. I am grateful to all of the above individuals. Selected archaeological site plans and photos (both pre- and post-publication) were provided by Paul Rainbird, John Valentin, Simon Hughes, Charlotte Coles, Naomi Payne and Sarnia Blackmore all of AC Archaeology and Neil Holbrook and Sarah Cobain of Cotswold Archaeology. Sean Taylor of the Cornwall Archaeological Unit provided a pre-publication plan from Trerank. David John of Bournemouth University supplied an image of Lake Farm fortress. My thanks also to Paul Cheetham formerly of Bournemouth University. My former colleague at Exeter Archaeology, Tony Ives, devised many of the plans relating to St Loye's college site and the *canabae* sites. Oly Martin, Rob Turner, Barbara Jupp and Kerry Peters supplied photos from their personal collections. Jonathan Newall undertook drone photography. I am thankful to all of them.

During the writing of the book I have received much encouragement from the citizens of Exeter including Simon Timms, Todd Gray, Tony Collings, Robin and Pamela Wootton, Sheila Rowe, Martin Weiler, Michael Leanza, Tim Hitchcock, Kevin Orton, Kevin Prout, Nestor Costa, Chris Gage, and Marcin Skovka; and from those beyond the walls, including Mark Stoye of Southampton University, John Collis at Sheffield University, Avril Sinclair, Michael Stone, Maggie Sheehy, Peter Barratt, Alan Dryland, Dave Sturge, and Dean Holden (ex-manager of Charlton Athletic FC).

The greatest level of personal support throughout the writing of the book has been from my wife Caroline and her mother, Mrs Cora Elizabeth McCullagh, for which I am eternally grateful.

Further reading

A major contribution in the study of Roman and Medieval Exeter arrived in 2021 with the publication of *Exeter: A Place in Time*: two volumes edited by Stephen Rippon and Neil Holbrook. The first volume provides a synthesis of the development of Exeter within a local, regional, national, and international context. The second volume presents a series of specialist contributions that underpin the general overview published in volume 1. The second volume also includes some detailed post-excavation analysis conducted on a selected number of Roman sites in Exeter which were excavated in the 1970s, but which had hitherto remained unpublished.

Roman Exeter and Topsham

Bidwell, P.T. and Boon, G.C. 1976. An antefix type of the Second Augustan Legion from Exeter, *Britannia* 7: 278-80.

Bidwell, P.T. 1979. *The Legionary Bath-House and Basilica and Forum at Exeter.* Exeter Archaeological Reports: Vol 1. Exeter: Exeter City Council and The University of Exeter.

Bidwell, P.T. 1980. *Roman Exeter: Fortress and Town.* Exeter: Exeter Museums.

Bidwell, P.T. 2021, The Legionary Fortress and its Landscape Context. In Rippon, S. and Holbrook, N. (eds): 2021a: 127-166.

Blaylock, S.R, 1995. *Exeter City Wall Survey. Exeter.* Exeter City Council.

Brown A. and Moorhead S. 2021. The Roman coins from Exeter and its Hinterland In Rippon, S. and Holbrook, N. (eds): 2021b: 127-166.

Dickinson, B. 1992. The samian potters' stamps. In Holbrook, N. and Bidwell, P.T. 1992: 50–4.

Fox, A. 1952. Roman Exeter *(Isca Dumnoniorum)*. Manchester: University Press.

Fox, A. 1968. Excavations at the South Gate, Exeter 1964-5, *Proceedings of the Devon Archaeological Society* 26: 1-20.

Garland, N. and Orellana, J. 2018. Prehistoric and Roman Occupation along the River Exe: Archaeological Investigations at the Aldi site, Exeter Road, Topsham, Devon, , *Proceedings of the Devon Archaeological Society* 76: 97-114.

Henderson, C.G. 1988. Exeter (*Isca Dumnoniorum*). In Webster G. (ed.): 91-119.

Henderson, C.G. 1991. Aspects in the planning of the Neronian fortress of *Legio II Augusta* at Exeter. In Maxfield, V.A. and Dobson M. J. (eds): 73-83.

Henderson, C.G. 1999. The design of the Neronian fortress baths at Exeter. In Delaine, J. and Johnston D.E. (eds): 164-83.

Henderson, C.G. 2001. The development of the South Gate at Exeter and its role in the city's defences. *Proceedings of the Devon Archaeological Society* 59: 45-123.

Holbrook, N. and Bidwell, P.T. 1991. *Roman Finds from Exeter.* Exeter Archaeological Reports Vol. 4. Exeter: Exeter City Council and The University of Exeter.

Holbrook, N. and Bidwell, P.T. 1992. Roman pottery from Exeter 1980–1990. In Perrin R. (ed.): *Journal of Roman Pottery Studies* 5: 35–80.

Holbrook, N, Orellana, J. and Randall, C. 2022. A new Roman fortification at St Sidwell's Point, Exeter: excavations in 2019. *Proceedings of the Devon Archaeological Society* 80: 77-102.

Jarvis, K. and Maxfield, V.A. 1975. The Excavation of a First-Century Roman Farmstead and a Late Neolithic Settlement, Topsham, Devon. *Proceedings of the Devon Archaeological Society* 33: 209-65.

Kaye, S. J. and Pamment Salvatore, J. 2022. Research on the effects of sea-level change on the River Exe estuary in the mid-1st century: implications for the location of Roman sea-port and barge-quay facilities serving the Neronian fortress of *Legio II Augusta* at Exeter. In Hodgson N. and Griffiths B. (eds): 187-200.

Macphail, R.I., Carey, C. and Allan, J. 2022. Contrasting use of space in post-Roman Exeter, UK; geoarchaeology of Dark Earth and medieval deposits below Exeter Cathedral. *Antiquity Project Gallery* 96 no. 386: 487–93.

Nash-Williams, V.E. 1929-32. The Problem of Roman Exeter. *Proceedings of the Devon Archaeological Exploration Society* I: 8-9.

Quinnell, H. 1984. Appendix 1: Excavations at the Stoke Hill Roman Signal Station, 1971. In Griffith, F.M. *Proceedings of the Devon Archaeological Society* 42: 28-30.

Quinnell, H. 2017. Prehistoric Exeter. *Proceedings of the Devon Archaeological Society* 75: 1-25.

Radford, C.A.R. 1937. Report of the Exeter Excavation Committee: The Roman site at Topsham. *Proceedings of the Devon Archaeological Exploration Society* III, part I: 4-23.

Rainbird, P. and Farnell A. 2019. A hint of Exeter's hinterland and port: A new large aisled hall building at Wessex Close, Topsham, Devon. *Britannia* 50: 385-93.

Reece, R. 1991. Roman Coins from Exeter. In Holbrook, N. and Bidwell, P.T. 1991: 33-38.

Rigby, V. 1991. Gaulish imports and related wares. In Holbrook, N. and Bidwell, P.T. 1991: 76–81.

Rippon, S. and Holbrook, N. (eds) 2021a. *Roman and Medieval Exeter and their hinterlands*, Exeter: A Place In Time 1. Oxford: Oxbow Books.

Rippon, S. and Holbrook, N. (eds) 2021b. *Studies in the Roman and Medieval Archaeology of Exeter*, Exeter: A Place In Time 2. Oxford: Oxbow Books.

Sage, A. and Allan, J. 2004. The Early Roman Military Defences, Late Roman Burials and Later Features at the Topsham School, Topsham. *Proceedings of the Devon Archaeological Society* 62: 1-39.

Salvatore, J.P. 2021. Roman military period activity beyond the *Porta Principalis Sinistra* (South Gate) of the Legionary Fortress at Exeter. *Proceedings of the Devon Archaeological Society* 79: 143-87.

Salvatore, J.P., Steinmetzer, M.F.R. and Quinnell, H. forthcoming. Prehistoric settlement remains, mid-1st century AD Roman settlement, Romano-British occupation and Late Roman burials at the former St. Loye's College, Topsham Road, Exeter. In *Roman Exeter: Devon Archaeological Society* Occasional Paper.

Shortt, W.T.P. 1840. *Sylva Antiqua Iscana*. London: J.B. Nichols and son.

Steinmetzer, M.F.R. Stead P., Pearce, P., Bidwell P. and Allan, J.P. forthcoming. Excavations at Princesshay, Exeter, 1997-2006. Part 1: Roman. In *Roman Exeter: Devon Archaeological Society* Occasional Paper.

Worth, R.N. 1891. Roman Devon. *Report of the Transactions of the Devonshire Association* 23: 25-101.

Other Roman military sites

Boon, C.G. 1987. *The Legionary Fortress at Caerleon-Isca: A brief account.*

Crummy, P. 1981. *Excavations at Lion Walk, Balkerne Lane, and Middleborough, Colchester Essex.* Colchester Archaeological Rep. 3. Colchester.

Griffith, F.M. 1984. Roman military sites in Devon: Some Recent Discoveries. *Proceedings of the Devon Archaeological Society* 42: 11-32.

Manning, W. H. 1981. *The Fortress Excavations 1968-1971.* Report on the Excavations at Usk 1965-1976. Cardiff. University of Wales Press.

Pitts, L.F. and St Joseph, J.K. 1985. *Inchtuthil: The Roman Legionary Fortress.* Britannia: Monograph Series No. 6. London (Society for the Promotion of Roman Studies).

Rainbird, P. and Caine, C.N. (forthcoming). An extra-mural settlement at the Okehampton Roman fort. *Proceedings of the Devon Archaeological Society.*

Russell, M., Cheetham, P. Stewart, D. and John, D. 2020. In the footsteps of Vespasian: rethinking the Roman legionary fortress at Lake Farm, Wimborne Minster. *Proceedings of the Dorset Natural History and Archaeological Society* 141: 111-120.

Smart, C. 2014. *A Roman Military Complex and Medieval Settlement on Church Hill, Calstock, Cornwall: Survey and Excavation 2007-2010.* British Archaeological Reports British Series 603.

Todd, M. 2007. Roman military occupation at Hembury (Devon). *Britannia* 38: 107-123.

Weddell, P.J., Reed, S.J. and Simpson, S.J. 1993. Excavation of the Exeter-Dorchester Roman road at the River Yarty and the Roman fort ditch and settlement site at Woodbury, near Axminster. *Proceedings of the Devon Archaeological Society* 51: 33-133.

Zienkiewicz, J. D. 1986. *The Legionary Fortress Baths at Caerleon*: 1 TheBuildings. Cardiff. CADW: Welsh Historic Monuments.

Roman Army

Anderson, J.D. 1992. *Roman Military Supply in North-East England,* BAR Brit. Ser. 224.

Bidwell, P.T. 1997. *Roman Forts in Britain.* London. B.T. Batsford.

Brewer, R J (ed.) 2000. *Roman Fortresses and their Legions.* The Society of Antiquaries and the National Museums and Galleries of Wales. Cardiff.

Brewer, R J (ed.) 2002. *The Second Augustan Legion and the Roman Military Machine.* National Museums and Galleries of Wales. Cardiff.

Davies, R. 1989. *Service in the Roman Army.* Edinburgh. Edinburgh University Press.

Gilliver, C.M. 2001. *The Roman Art of War.* Stroud. The History Press.

Holbrook, N. and Shiel, N. 2002. A Claudian Coin Hoard from Roborough, Devon. *Proceedings of the Devon Archaeological Society* 60: 215-18.

Jones, M.J. 1975. Roman Fort Defences to A.D. 117. British Archaeological Reports 21.

Jones, R. H. 2012. *Roman Camps in Britain.* Amberley Publishing. Stroud.

Luttwak, E. N. 1999. *The Grand Strategy of the Roman Empire: From the first century A.D. to the third.* London. Weidenfeld and Nicholson.

Manning, W. H. 2002. Early Roman Campaigns in the South-West of Britain. In Brewer, R. J. (ed.) 2000, 27-44.

Mason, D.J.P. 1988: 'Prata Legionis in Britain', *Britannia* 19: 163-89.

Shirley, E. 2001. *Building a Roman Legionary Fortress.* Stroud. Tempus Publishing.

Sommer, C.S. 2006. Military *vici* in Roman Britain revisited. In Wilson, R.J.A. (ed.) 2006, 95-146.

Smart, C. and Fonte, J. (in preparation): The disposition of the Roman army west of Exeter: a reassessment of evidence from the Taw Valley, Devon.

Taylor, S R, 2023. St Austell to A30 Link Road, Cornwall: Archaeological Mitigation Interim Report, Cornwall Archaeological Unit. Truro.

General Roman

Allason-Jones, L. 2005. *Women in Roman Britain.* York. The Council for British Archaeology.

Allen, D. (with Taylor, M., and Hill D.) 2023. Experiments in Early Window Glass: Four Production Methods and Their Possible Use in Roman Britain. *Journal of Glass Studies* 65.

Birley, A.R. 2005. *The Roman Government of Britain.* Oxford. Oxford University Press.

de la Bédoyère, G. 1991. *The Buildings of Roman Britain.* London. Batsford.

DeLaine, J and Johnston, D.E. (eds). 1999. Roman Baths and Bathing. *Proceedings   of the First International Conference on Roman Baths, Vol. 2 Design and Construction, Journal of Roman Archaeology* Supplement 37. Portsmouth.

Driessen, M. and Besselsen, E. 2014. *Voorburg-Arentsburg: a Roman Harbour Town between Rhine and Meuse* (Netherlands). University of Amsterdam.

Esmonde Cleary, A. S., 1989. *The Ending of Roman Britain.*

Fulford, M. and Holbrook, N. (eds) 2015: *The Towns of Roman Britain: The Contribution of Commercial Archaeology Since 1990.* Britannia Monograph Series No. 27.

Hodgson, N. and Griffiths, B. (eds). 2022. *Roman Frontier Archaeology - in Britain and Beyond.* Archaeopress Roman Archaeology 92. Oxford. Archaeopress.

Holbrook, N., 2015. The towns of South-West England. In Fulford, M. and Holbrook, N. (eds): 90-116.

Maxfield, V.A. and Dobson M.J. (eds). 1991. Roman Frontier Studies 1989. *Proceedings of the XVth International Congress of Roman Frontier Studies.* Exeter. University of Exeter Press.

Millett, M. 1992: *The Romanization of Britain.* Cambridge. Cambridge University Press.

Parcero-Oubina, C., Smart, C. and Fonte, J., 2023. Remote Sensing and GIS Modelling of Roman Roads in South West Britain. *Journal of Computer Applications in Archaeology* 6(1): 62–78. DOI: https://doi.org/10.5334/jcaa.109

Toller, H. 2014. The Roman Road from Dorchester to Exeter. *Proceedings of the Devon Archaeological Society*: 72, 103-130.

Tomlin, R.S.O. 2016. *Roman London's first voices: writing tablets from the Bloomberg excavations 2010-14.* Museum of London Archaeology Monograph 72. London.

Wacher, J.S. (ed.) 1975. *The Civitas Capitals of Roman Britain.* Leicester. Leicester University Press.

Webster, G. (ed.) 1988. *Fortress into City. The Consolidation of Roman Britain, First Century AD.* London. B.T. Batsford.

Webster, G. 1993. *Boudica; the British revolt against Rome AD 60.* London. B.T. Batsford

Wilson, R.J.A. (ed.) 2006. Romanitas: Essays on Roman Archaeology in Honour of Sheppard Frere on the Occasion of his Ninetieth Birthday. Oxford Oxbow Books.

Ancient Sources

Dio Cassius *(Roman History)*, Suetonius *(The Lives of the Twelve Ceasars)*, Tacitus *(Annals, Roman History*, and *Agricola)*, Ovid *(Fasti)* and Eusebius *(Life of Constantine)* have all been translated into English in the Loeb Classical Library volumes.

Pseudo-Hyginus *(de munitionibus castrorum)* and Polybius *(Excursion on the Roman camp)* may be found in translation in Miller, M.C.J. and DeVoto J.G. 1994. *Fortification of the Roman Camp.* Ares Publishers. Chicago.

THINGS TO SEE AND DO IN ROMAN EXETER

The Royal Albert Memorial Museum (RAMM) in Queen Street has on display some of the finds mentioned in this book including the face of a gorgon which once sat on the roof of a bathhouse, the cup upon which Lucius Julius Hipponicus scratched his name so that it wouldn't get lost, and the glass vessel from Topsham depicting a chariot race in which Crescens defeated Pyramus. The Museum is open Tuesdays to Sundays from 10.00-17.00. Check the website www.rammuseum.org.uk.

The faced Roman wall to its full height is shown in the photo taken at Quay Lane (opposite bottom right). To get there first go to the bottom of South Street, where the tower of the South Gate of the Roman city is marked out on the ground, and then go over the footbridge which takes you on top of the wall before descending the steps down to Quay Lane. For a more detailed exploration of the wall you can follow the Exeter City Wall Trail by visiting the nine information boards set up around the city. Alternatively, Exeter City Council offers a wide variety of free Red Coat guided tours throughout the year. The City Wall tour takes place twice a week during the summer months (1st April - 31st October) and lasts two hours. For the Winter Programme and to check all tour information, please look online at www.visitexeter.com. This website also has a downloadable map of the City Wall Trail. The museum in Topsham has a dedicated Roman display. The musuem opens on Wednesdays to Sundays from 2-5pm during the months of April to October. Check online at www.topshammuseum.org.uk for further details.

Roman military re-enactment groups are drawn to Exeter due to its origin as the fortress of the Second Augustan Legion and you may be lucky enough to encounter a patrolling Roman legionary. At the Catherine Street Almshouses, just off the High Street, an information board tells the story of the fortress defences and a later Roman town house which stood on the same site. A mosaic from this house survived only because it had subsided into the centuries old ditch of the legionary defences which had long been forgotten when the house was built.

Photos and images opposite: clockwise from top left:
Re-enactor Oly Martin at the Catherine Street Almshouses' information board (photo by the author).
Legionaries from Isca Romano form up outside the Cathedral (photo: Nigel Cheffers-Heard).
Image of a mid-fourth century mother and daughter spinning wool (© Graham Sumner).
A Red Coat Guide tells visitors about the Roman wall (photo: Kerry Peters, Exeter City Council).
Finds on display at the Royal Albert Memorial Museum (© RAMM).
Image of a mid-first century legionary on the march (© Graham Sumner).
The central image shows a wall-plaque in Cathedral Close which celebrates the birth of the city of Exeter around AD 80 (photo by the author).

To the west of the
Cathedral lie buried the remains of the
bathhouse of the Roman Second Augustan Legion built c AD 60,
replaced c AD 80 by the basilica and forum of the new town
ISCA DUMNONIORUM which remained until the 5th century.
An Anglo-Saxon minster stood here from the 7th century,
elevated to cathedral status in 1050.

✝   ✝   ✝

Index